MEDIEVAL GLASS

for Popes, Princes, and Peasants

David Whitehouse

WITH CONTRIBUTIONS BY

William Gudenrath
and Karl Hans Wedepohl

THE CORNING MUSEUM OF GLASS, CORNING, NEW YORK

This publication accompanies the exhibition "Medieval Glass for Popes, Princes, and Peasants," held at The Corning Museum of Glass, May 15, 2010–January 2, 2011.

EDITOR
Richard W. Price

DESIGN AND TYPOGRAPHY
Jacolyn S. Saunders

PHOTOGRAPHY
Nicholas L. Williams, Andrew M. Fortune, Allison S. Lavine, and Martin J. Pierce

RESEARCHER AND PROOFREADER
Mary B. Chervenak

RIGHTS AND REPRODUCTIONS
Jill Thomas-Clark

REFERENCE LIBRARIAN
Gail P. Bardhan

All of the photographs in this book are by The Corning Museum of Glass (Nicholas L. Williams and Andrew M. Fortune), unless otherwise specified in the "Picture Credits" section.

COVER IMAGE
Hedwig beaker, blown (perhaps in mold), wheel-cut. Place of manufacture uncertain, perhaps Sicily, late 12th century. H. 8.7 cm, D. about 7.1 cm. The Corning Museum of Glass (67.1.11).

Contents

Preface

FOR MANY OF US, the words "medieval glass" are synonymous with the extraordinary stained glass windows that transform the interiors of so many European churches of the later Middle Ages. This book—like the exhibition—has a different focus. It is a selective introduction to medieval glass vessels, made in the course of more than 1,000 years, that were intended for use and display: for eating and drinking, lighting, worship, science, and medicine. The book examines the history of medieval glass vessels, explores how some of them were made, and explains how, by determining the composition of glass, the chemist makes a valuable contribution to our understanding of developments in glassmaking in the Middle Ages. These chapters are followed by a catalog of 124 glass vessels, mostly from western Europe, that range in date between the fifth and 16th centuries. At the end of the book are a bibliography of works cited in the text and an index.

I am delighted to pay tribute to the support of the directors and staff of the museums in the United States and Europe that lent objects to the exhibition, all of which are described in these pages; the names of the individuals and institutions appear in the Acknowledgments on page 5. I am particularly grateful to the architect Karl Amendt of Krefeld, Germany, who lent no fewer than 39 objects from his personal collection, and to Dr. Dedo von Kerssenbrock-Krosigk, director of the Glasmuseum Hentrich in the Museum Kunst Palast, Düsseldorf, where the Amendt Collection is usually displayed.

The chapters on the techniques used by medieval glassmakers and the contribution of chemical analyses to our understanding of changes in the composition of glass made at different times and in different places were written by William Gudenrath, resident adviser at The Studio of The Corning Museum of Glass, and Karl Hans Wedepohl, a retired professor and former director of the Institute of Geochemistry at the University of Göttingen respectively. Working with them has been a pleasure.

The names of staff members of The Corning Museum of Glass who were responsible for the creation of the book and the exhibition appear on page 5.

David Whitehouse
Executive Director
The Corning Museum of Glass

Acknowledgments

THE OBJECTS illustrated in this book and displayed in the exhibition belong to individuals and museums in the United States and Europe. We thank the following friends and colleagues for their generosity in making their treasures available:

Karl Amendt, Krefeld.

Diözesanmuseum Freising: Sylvia Hahn, director.

Glasmuseum Hentrich, Stiftung Museum Kunst Palast, Düsseldorf: Dedo von Kerssenbrock-Krosigk, director.

Grand Curtius, Glass Department, Liège: Jean-Paul Philippart, director.

Landesmuseum Württemberg, Stuttgart: Cornelia Ewigleben, director; Sabine Hesse.

The Metropolitan Museum of Art, New York: Thomas P. Campbell, director; Andrew Burnet, Carlos Picón, and Lisa Pilosi.

Musée des Beaux-Arts, Chartres: Nadine Berthelier, director; Valérie Dufresne.

Musée du Louvre, Paris: Henri Loyrette, director; Sophie Makariou and Isabelle Luche.

Musei Vaticani, Vatican City: Antonio Paolucci, director.

Museum für Angewandte Kunst Frankfurt: Ulrich Schneider, director; Stephan von der Schulenburg and Sandra Schwartz.

Museum für Kunst und Gewerbe, Hamburg: Sabine Schulze, director; Christine Kitzlinger.

Museum zu Allerheiligen, Schaffhausen: Roger Fayet, director; Ariane Dannacher.

Rheinisches Landesmuseum Bonn: Gabriele Uelsberg, director; Eva Gebhard and Marion Nickel.

Statens Historiska Museum, Stockholm: Lars Amréus, director; Gunnar Andersson and Mari-Louise Franzén.

We also acknowledge the dedication of the staff of The Corning Museum of Glass responsible for preparing this book and mounting the exhibition:

Conservation: Stephen Koob and Astrid van Giffen.

Education: Amy Schwartz.

Exhibition design: Robert Cassetti and Brian Jones.

Librarians: Gail Bardhan and Beth Hylen.

Photography: Nicholas Williams, Andrew Fortune, Allison Lavine, and Martin Pierce.

Preparators: Stephen Hazlett, Fritz Ochab, and Stefan Zoller.

Publications: Richard Price and Jacolyn Saunders.

Registrar's office: Warren Bunn, Brandy Harold, Christy Cook, and Melissa White.

Rights and reproductions: Jill Thomas-Clark and Mary Chervenak.

The Studio: William Gudenrath.

Introduction

THE PURPOSES of this Introduction are four: (1) to provide a bare-bones summary of the background against which medieval glassmaking developed; (2) to note how, while glassmakers were producing simple objects for everyday use, the unique properties of glass became the stuff of legends and literature; (3) to describe how the study of medieval glass vessels has evolved in the last hundred years; and (4) to offer, on page 20, an outline of the glass vessels that appear in the catalog on pages 88–255.

THE BACKGROUND[1]

The Middle Ages is the name given to the period of European history between the eclipse of ancient Rome in the fifth century A.D. and the dawn of the Renaissance in 15th-century Italy. During the 1,000 years of the Middle Ages, Europe underwent profound changes. Institutions such as Roman law and the Church survived, while political and economic systems atrophied before enjoying a gradual revival.

Throughout western Europe, the fourth and fifth centuries were a time of transformation. Roman imperial government collapsed and was replaced by smaller political entities with less centralized authority and simpler economies.

Roman civilization was firmly rooted in the Mediterranean region, and the expansion of that civilization beyond the Alps created a vast reservoir of revenue, raw materials, and manpower for the heartland of the empire. At the same time, this expansion introduced the first truly urban society north of the Alps, together with widely based communications, comprehensive monetary systems, a legal code, ambitious engineering, and literacy. Roman expansion changed the face of Europe almost as dramatically as European expansion changed the face of the preindustrial Americas a millennium and a half later.

As the Roman Empire declined, the frontiers were withdrawn toward the Mediterranean. The causes of the decline were various, and they have been debated for centuries. Pressure of immigrants from outside the northern and eastern borders, internal conflict provoked by the absence of an accepted process of succession to the throne, demographic decline, and pandemic disease have all been invoked as factors in the fall of Rome. Whatever combination

Detail (showing prunted beaker) from the Codex Manesse, a collection of songs compiled between about 1300 and 1340, probably for the patrician Manesse family of Zurich. Heidelberg University Library (Cod. Pal. Germ. 848, f.80).

1. Much of what follows is based on articles in *The New Encyclopaedia Britannica*, Chicago: Encyclopaedia Britannica Inc., 1997, v. 18, pp. 605–632, that provide a comprehensive overview of European medieval history and culture.

of events caused the disintegration of Rome's western provinces, in the early fourth century Emperor Constantine (r. 306–337) moved the imperial capital from Rome to Constantinople in the eastern Mediterranean. The division of the Roman Empire into western and eastern realms, instituted by Emperor Diocletian (r. 284–305), was complete.

The Migration Period

A foretaste of the Migration Period (A.D. 350–550), during which "barbarian" peoples settled in many of the former provinces in Europe and the western Mediterranean, occurred in the late third century, when Roman territories around the North Sea came under pressure. The first mass immigration from beyond the imperial frontier appeared in the east. The Goths crossed the border and defeated a Roman army at Adrianople (modern Edirne) in 378. Later, in 410, they sacked Rome, and the last Roman emperor in the west, Romulus Augustulus, was deposed by a Gothic king in 476.

Migrations also disrupted the northern provinces. Roman governors tried to protect their provinces by settling immigrants in frontier regions to provide buffers against further pressure from outside. Eventually, however, the Franks migrated into Gaul, where Clovis became their first king in 481. Meanwhile, Angles, Saxons, and Jutes settled in England, and before the end of the fifth century, the Lombards moved into Italy. Thus, by 500, large parts of the western Roman Empire were ruled by kings who were not and never claimed to be Roman citizens.

Although the Germanic peoples were pagan at the time of the migrations, many of them became Christian in the course of the next century, and eventually the pope and the king of the Franks formed a powerful alliance.

The Church was instrumental in forging political unity in Europe, and it preserved learning and literacy. Monasteries, which proliferated especially after Saint Benedict compiled his Rule, required a strict daily routine of prayer, manual labor, and study.

Urban society throughout Europe collapsed in the early Middle Ages. Rome, for example, shrank from a city with an estimated population of more than 1,000,000 in the first century A.D. to a few tens of thousands in the seventh century. Although cities were now small, many of them remained the seats of bishops.

The Expansion of Islam and the Carolingian Renaissance

In the 630s and 640s, the followers of the prophet Muhammad advanced from Arabia, occupied large areas of the eastern Roman Empire, and destroyed the empire of the Sasanians in Iraq, Iran, and parts of Central Asia, all in the name of a new religion, Islam. They also advanced along the coast of North Africa, and in 711 they invaded Spain.

The Arab invasion of southern Europe was halted, in France, by the Frankish king Charles Martel (the Hammer) in 732 or 733. Shortly after his victory, Charles became king and formed an alliance with the pope, who was fighting the Lombards in Italy. This was the beginning of the Carolingian dynasty. Charles's son, also named Charles and later identified as Charlemagne (Charles the Great), was described by one of his contemporaries as "the father of Europe." The coronation of Charlemagne by Pope Leo III on Christmas Day 800 marked the beginning of the Holy Roman Empire. Much of Europe was now united politically under an emperor who fostered a flowering of intellectual life that is often described as the "Carolingian Renaissance."

The Age of the Vikings

While the Carolingian dynasty (750–887) and its successors, the Ottonians (919–1024), ruled much of continental Europe, the Vikings wielded power in Scandinavia. "Vikings" is the collective name for explorers, settlers, merchants, and raiders from Norway, Sweden, and Denmark who were active in many parts of Europe and the North Atlantic between the late eighth and early 11th centuries.

Eyewitnesses around the coasts of the North Sea and beyond recorded with horror the bloodthirsty raids of Vikings in search of booty. Time after time, they reported that villages were burned and monasteries stripped of their treasures.

But this was not the whole story. In their famous longships, Viking settlers voyaged as far west as Iceland, Greenland, and even Newfoundland in Canada. The settlement in Canada was short-lived and the colonies in Greenland were eventually abandoned, but descendants of the Vikings still inhabit Iceland. And the Normans, who invaded England in 1066, were descendants of Vikings who established an independent state in northwestern France.

Meanwhile, Viking merchants traveled along the Volga River to the Black Sea, and Viking mercenaries formed the emperor's Varangian Guard in Constantinople. Medieval chroniclers wrote of Viking activities in Spain, in Italy, and along the coast of North Africa.

At home in Scandinavia and northwestern Germany, the Viking merchants created trading centers such as Haithabu and Birka, where archeologists have recovered artifacts from many parts of Europe and the Middle East, including vast numbers of silver coins minted at Baghdad and other Islamic cities, as well as glass vessels from all over Europe. Indeed, some of the best-preserved glasses of the period between 800 and 1000 were discovered in Viking graves.

The Medieval Church

The early Christian Church was organized in dioceses administered by bishops. By the end of the eighth century, the organization had expanded, and adjoining dioceses were grouped in provinces under the authority of archbishops appointed by the pope. Within the diocese, over time, a system of parishes developed, each served by a local priest. By the end of the Middle Ages, many parishes were controlled by monasteries, the greatest of which became substantial landowners.

Church and state became interdependent, the Church relying on the protection of the king, and the king receiving confirmation of his secular authority from the Church. Many members of the king's administration were priests. Archbishops and bishops often became major landowners. Occasional conflicts apart, this symbiosis of Church and state continued throughout the Middle Ages. Meanwhile, the power of the papacy grew, so that in the 13th and 14th centuries, the government of the Church was centralized in Rome and its structure was emphatically hierarchical.

Saints were revered by the faithful, and containers known as reliquaries were used to hold their relics (that is, parts of their bodies or objects associated with them). (See pages 55–56.)

Agrarian Society

Throughout the Middle Ages, even after the revival of cities (see below), most of the population lived on the land and crops produced most of the basic foodstuffs. In the Mediterranean region, the lighter soils supported an economy based on the cultivation of grain, vines, and olives, while in Germany and other parts of western Europe the heavier soils were well suited to growing cereals, legumes, and other vegetables. On higher ground throughout Europe, a largely pastoral economy, based on cattle, sheep, and goats, flourished.

In western Europe and England, the heavy soil required good drainage and the use of oxen for plowing. This led to planting the crops in slightly raised strips separated by shallow drainage ditches. These open fields, consisting of "ridge and furrow" patterns of plowing, became characteristic of a large area extending across Germany to the British Isles, as did the "three-field" system of maintaining soil fertility by crop rotation: in any field, cereals were planted in the first year of the cycle, nitrogen-rich legumes in the second, and nothing in the third.

Throughout rural Europe, in addition to personal relationships, social organization was based on land tenure. Lords granted land to subordinates in return for specific goods and services. In this feudal society, landlords exercised many of the functions we associate with the state's administration. Indeed, the feudal system tended to reduce the central authority of the king by dividing authority among the feudal landlords. This tendency was reversed from the 12th century onward by the centralization of the state and the growth of cities and city-based power.

In 1347–1350, Europe was devastated by the Black Death, a pandemic plague that, together with subsequent outbreaks, killed an estimated one-third of the population. The Black Death afflicted all branches of society, but its impact on agriculture, which depended on intensive labor by large numbers of peasants, was particularly severe.

The Revival of Towns and Trade

Urban life, commercial activity, and long-distance trade began to revive in the Mediterranean region and around the Baltic and North Seas by the 11th century. In Italy, cities such as Venice,

Pisa, and Genoa were developing on the basis of maritime trade with the eastern Mediterranean. By the 13th century, Florence had an estimated population of 200,000, based largely on textile production. Elsewhere in Europe, as trade intensified, cities in the Baltic region, such as Lübeck and Hamburg, formed the powerful Hanseatic League to promote and protect commerce.

At that time, stronger nation states, wealthy cities, and extensive commercial networks were beginning to change the face of Europe. They emerged unevenly, at different times, and in differing degrees. But the fabric of the preindustrial world was taking shape.

The Crusades

The Crusades were one aspect of the increasing contact between Christian Europe and the predominantly Muslim Near East, and the establishment of temporary European control over parts of the Levant facilitated commercial relations and the transmission of technical knowledge from east to west.

The Crusades were military expeditions aimed at wresting control of Jerusalem and the Christian shrine of the Holy Sepulcher from the Muslims. The First Crusade was launched in 1095, and the last in 1270. The First Crusade began as a response to an appeal by the Byzantine emperor for military assistance against the Turks, who were encroaching on Byzantine territory in Anatolia. Pope Urban II called for a Christian army not only to fight the Turks but also to capture the Holy Sepulcher, which was a major center for Christian pilgrimage. In 1099, the crusaders occupied Jerusalem.

In the Second Crusade, the pope assembled an army to oppose the Turkish ruler Zangī, who in 1144 captured Edessa, a city in Syria, from the crusaders. The pope's army was destroyed at the Battle of Hattin in 1187 by the Muslim leader Saladin, who recaptured Jerusalem. Shocked by the fall of Jerusalem, Pope Gregory VIII launched the Third Crusade in 1189. Two years later, the crusaders captured Acre, a major port, but failed to take Jerusalem. However, a peace was concluded with the Muslims, one of the terms of which was access to the Holy Sepulcher for Christian pilgrims.

The Fourth Crusade was intended to be an attack on Egypt, but ended in the conquest of Constantinople in 1204, an event that put an end to any hope of an alliance between the Roman and Byzantine churches. Several more crusades took place in the 13th century, culminating in the catastrophic Eighth Crusade, when disease annihilated the Christian army and killed its leader, King Louis IX of France.

Markets, Fairs, and Guilds

Greater political stability and an increase in specialized production led to growth in the volume of goods exchanged. For example, wool and cloth were produced in the well-drained regions of western Europe that were suitable for raising sheep and for wine production, especially around the Mediterranean but also along the Rhine River.

Figure 1
Man with two goblets and a pitcher outside a makeshift tavern (upper
right). Detail from a miniature showing a bishop blessing the Lendit
Fair at La Plaine, between Paris and Saint-Denis (mid-15th century).
Bibliothèque Nationale, Paris (Ms. Lat. 962, f.264).

Apart from barter between individual members of the community, which was particularly
common in rural areas, exchange took place in three different kinds of contexts: between
buyers and retailers with permanent premises in the cities, at local markets, and at regional
and international fairs. City-based markets, which took place at regular intervals (often week-
ly), attracted suppliers of produce grown and gathered in the surrounding countryside, as
well as retailers of manufactured goods. These events left a lasting impression on the topog-
raphy of many European cities, where the market square is still a feature of the townscape.

Fairs were different in scale and scope. They took place at less frequent but equally regular
intervals (Fig. 1), and the largest of them attracted merchants from all over Europe. Some of
the best-known international fairs were held in northern France, where the counts of Champagne derived much of their wealth from taxes levied on merchants attending the fairs of
Provins, Troyes, and other cities.

Guilds were associations of merchants and craftsmen that were formed to support and
protect their members and to promote their professional interests. They came into existence
as city life expanded in and after the 10th century, and they flourished in Europe between the
11th and 16th centuries, when they played important roles in social and economic life.

These guilds fell into two groups. *Merchant* guilds were associations of wholesale or retail, local or long-distance traders in a city who dealt in a particular category of goods. Merchant tailors, for example, dealt in clothes. Merchant guilds regulated their members' activities and were recognized by city governments. *Craft* guilds, which began soon after the merchants' associations, united craftsmen according to their various branches of production: blacksmiths, leatherworkers, bakers, and glassmakers.

Each of these guilds established its own code of conduct to govern competition among members, and it negotiated with the government. Craft guilds also provided training for apprentices and encouraged their development into master craftsmen. The glassmakers of Venice are a perfect, and well-documented, example of a successful guild of craftsmen.

Glass in Science and Medicine

In the 12th and 13th centuries, scholarship was stimulated as Latin translations of books written by ancient Greek and Muslim scientists began to circulate in Europe. Science and medicine were two fields that derived a direct benefit from advances in glassmaking. The transparent and noncorrosive nature of glass made it ideal for use in scientific experiments. One piece of glass apparatus that was vital to work in alchemy (medieval science) was the still. Glass flasks were employed in uroscopy to diagnose disease based on the color of urine. The increasing use of glass also led to the emergence of optics as a branch of science and to the development of lenses. (See pages 60–61.)

GLASS IN LEGENDS AND LITERATURE

Glass not only furnished households and taverns with vessels for eating and drinking, and churches and cathedrals with richly colored pictorial windows; from time to time, its remarkable properties also stimulated the imaginations of visionaries, poets, and storytellers. Long before the Middle Ages, extraordinary phenomena had been described in terms of glass. In the Book of Revelation, written in the first century A.D., Saint John described the signs that preceded the battle of Armageddon. Here is one of them: "Then I saw another sign in heaven, great and marvelous, seven angels who had the seven last plagues, because in them the wrath of God is finished. And I saw something like a sea of glass mixed with fire, and those who had been victorious over the beast and his image and the number of his name, standing on the sea of glass, holding the harps of God" (Rev. 15:1, 2). The angels on the sea of glass appear in Figure 2, which reproduces a page in a 15th-century manuscript in the Wellcome Library, London.

The Qur'an also contains an account of remarkable glass. It relates (in Sura 27:20–44) how the hoopoe, a brightly colored bird, told Solomon about Bilqīs, the queen of Sheba, a sun-worshiper who possessed a remarkable throne. Solomon instructed one of his jinns (genies) to bring him the throne, and, hoping to convert Bilqīs, he invited her to visit him. When she

Figure 2
Those who had conquered the beast, standing on a sea of glass (Rev. 15:2).
Illustration from a manuscript of the Book of Revelation and other works
(about 1420–1430). Wellcome Library, London (WMS 49, f.19r).

entered Solomon's palace, Bilqīs saw what she thought was a pool of water, and in tucking up her dress to prevent it from getting wet, she uncovered her legs. Solomon removed the cause of her embarrassment by explaining, "This is but a palace paved smooth with slabs of glass."

In medieval Europe, stories of amazing deeds and heroic exploits surrounded the figure of Alexander the Great. The Alexander Romance is the generic name of numerous collections of stories about Alexander. The earliest version of the Alexander Romance dates from the third century A.D. Throughout late antiquity and the Middle Ages, the Romance was expanded and revised to contain new myths about the life and times of Alexander. Medieval versions exist in several European languages as well as in Middle Eastern languages and Ethiopic. One popular myth tells how Alexander was lowered from a ship in a glass barrel to observe the wonders of the sea. Figure 3 reproduces a miniature painting in a 15th-century French version of the Alexander Romance. The picture shows Alexander, wearing his crown, looking at fish through the transparent walls of his barrel. Such was the popularity of the Alexander Romance that, toward the end of the 14th century, Geoffrey Chaucer (about 1342–1400) makes the Monk apologize for recounting the stories in *The Canterbury Tales*.

The most celebrated poet of the Middle Ages, Dante Alighieri (1265–1321), repeatedly emphasized a point by comparing his experience or observation to glass (Toynbee 1903). For example, in a passage in book 24 of the *Purgatorio*, Dante conveyed an impression of the radiant aspect of the Angel in the sixth Circle of Purgatory as follows:

Giammai non si videro in furnace

Vetri o metallic sì lucent e rossi

(Never did one see in a furnace glass or metal so bright and red).

Later, in book 27, Dante describes how, after Virgil had persuaded him to enter the fiery zone of the seventh Circle, he encountered such intense heat that he would have plunged into molten glass to cool himself:

Come fui dentro, in un bogliente vetro

Gittato mi sarei per rinfrescarmi,

Tant'era ivi lo incendio senza metro

(When I was inside, I would have thrown myself into molten glass to refresh myself, so great was the immeasurable fire there).

Figure 3

Alexander the Great being lowered from a ship in a glass barrel. From a French translation of the Alexander Romance. The manuscript was presented to Margaret of Anjou, wife of King Henry VI of England, by the earl of Shrewsbury. France, Rouen, about 1445. The British Library, London (Royal 15 E. VI, f.20v).

Dante also refers to ordinary, transparent glass. Thus, in book 3 of the *Convivio*, he uses glass to explain the nature of eyesight: "Le cose visibili vengono dentro all'occhio—non dico le cose, ma le forme loro—per lo mezzo diafano, non realmente, ma intenzionalmente, siccome quasi in vetro transparente" (Visible things enter the eye—not the things [themselves] but their forms—through the diaphanous medium, as through transparent glass).

THE STUDY OF MEDIEVAL GLASS VESSELS

The study of glass vessels of the Middle Ages began in two entirely separate ways. (The study of stained glass followed a third, art-historical trajectory.) By the late 19th century, antiquarians in northern Europe had enjoyed a long tradition of collecting and studying the material remains of the Migration Period, the time when tribes of "barbarians" from outside the frontiers of the Roman Empire migrated into the former Roman provinces and established small but independent kingdoms. The Angles and Saxons, for example, settled in the former provinces of Britannia and created Anglo-Saxon England.

Among most of these groups, it was customary to bury the dead in single graves accompanied by personal possessions: a few simple items for ordinary people, and larger, more opulent assemblages for the elite. If cremation was practiced, the burned bones were usually placed in an earthenware vessel, and these, too, might be accompanied by artifacts. The jewelry, tools, weapons, and utensils (including glass) that came to light when farmers and construction workers chanced upon early medieval cemeteries provided antiquarians with objects for the study of the material culture of their remote ancestors, whose history and customs were poorly recorded in written documents and whose buildings, mostly of wood, hardly ever survived. Originally, therefore, the study of early medieval glass vessels was essentially the study of objects recovered from cemeteries.

While antiquarians were collecting vessels found in early medieval cemeteries, first by chance and later by chance and by planned excavations, students were paying increasingly greater attention to examples of the "minor arts" of the later Middle Ages—not only glass but also ceramics, small metal objects, and so on—that had survived above ground. Some of these objects, such as liturgical vessels and reliquaries made of precious metal, had always been famous, while others were recognized only in modern times as being hundreds of years old. Two sources of information that were rarely available to students of early medieval glass vessels provided information about late medieval objects: images of glass vessels (and other things) in medieval paintings and other works of art (Figs. 4 and 5), some of which could be attributed to specific dates and places, and references to glasses (and occasionally to glassmaking) in inventories and other documents.

These two strands—the antiquarian or archeological study of early medieval glass and the study of later medieval vessels—were brought together by Albert Hartshorne, whose *Old English Glasses* appeared in 1897 (Hartshorne 1897). This is a copiously illustrated narrative account of the history of glass drinking vessels, mostly but by no means entirely from

Figure 4
Tavern scene with men drinking from bottles and beakers, with a cellarer below.
Illustration from a "Treatise on the Vices" produced in Genoa (late 14th century).
The British Library, London (Ms. Add. 27695, f.14).

Figure 5
Bottle. William the Conqueror and his companions feast before the Battle of Hastings in 1066. The inscription, "HIC EPISCOPVS CIBV ET POTV BENE-DICIT," means "Here [i.e., in this image] the bishop blessed the food and drink." Here, a servant holds up a transparent container, presumably glass, containing a dark liquid, probably wine. Detail from the Bayeux Tapestry (between 1066 and about 1100, perhaps before 1077). Musée de la Tapisserie Bayeux, Bayeux.

England. Hartshorne's description of Anglo-Saxon glass begins with a review of the scant written evidence and continues with a survey of finds from pagan cemeteries. On the other hand, all later glasses, both from the Continent and from England, are objects that survived above ground because they were treated as heirlooms, objects of rarity or beauty, or containers of holy relics. Hartshorne's account of post-medieval glass is supported by nearly 80 pages of original documents.

The most comprehensive account of late medieval glass vessels made in Europe, based mainly on objects that have survived above ground and on descriptions and illustrations in manuscripts of that period, is Franz Rademacher's *Die deutschen Gläser des Mittelalters* (German glass of the Middle Ages) of 1933 (Rademacher 1933). The author used all of these sources, together with objects recovered from the ground largely by chance, to provide a panorama of 14th- and 15th-century glass vessels—from bottles and related forms to lamps and glasses for drinking.

Then, especially after World War II, archeologists began to turn their attention to the buried remains of the Middle Ages as well as those of the pre-Roman and Roman periods. Archeologists in Scandinavia and other parts of northern Europe had been carefully excavating the remains of their medieval past for several generations, but it was only in the second half of the 20th century that "medieval archeology" became established all over Europe. We can almost plot the emergence of groups of professional and amateur archeologists focusing on the Middle Ages by noting where and when scholarly periodical literature appeared first: volume one of *Medieval Archaeology* was published in the United Kingdom in 1957, the first issue of *Archéologie Médiévale* came out in France in 1971, and the first volume of the Italian journal *Archeologia Medievale* appeared in 1974.

The study of medieval glass vessels underwent a similar development. The medieval (non–stained glass) sections of the check lists of recent publications that appeared annually in the *Journal of Glass Studies*, published by The Corning Museum of Glass, contained just seven entries in 1967 and 11 in 1971. Thereafter the number grew rapidly: 18 in 1973, 28 in 1975, and 46 in 1977. In the 1990s, the number of entries varied between 50 and 63. The numbers of papers published in the triennial *Annales* of the International Association for the History of Glass tell much the same story. Contributions on Roman subjects outnumbered those on the medieval period by 10 to one in 1967, but thereafter (except in 1973 and 1995) the numbers have been comparable.

In the 1980s, three major exhibitions drew attention to our new appreciation of the skills of the medieval glassmaker. In 1987, the Amendt Collection of medieval glass was exhibited in Rotterdam and Düsseldorf; the following year, "Phönix aus Sand und Asche" (Phoenix from sand and ash) was shown in Bonn and Basel; and in 1989–1990, "A travers le verre" (Through glass) was displayed in Rouen. More recent publications include Stiaffini (1999), a survey of medieval glass and glassmaking in Italy, and Price (2000) and Tyson (2000), which together survey glass of the period between about 350 and 1500 found in England. The glass of medieval Europe has never been studied more extensively and in greater detail than it is today, and both this book and the exhibition it accompanies do no more than scratch the surface and—I hope—whet one's appetite to see and learn more about this subject.

The history of the study of medieval glass vessels has affected the way they have been collected in North America. Few later medieval vessels entered American museums until relatively recently, an unusual exception being a group of beakers from the Crimea (catalog numbers 46–49) that were donated to The Metropolitan Museum of Art in New York City in 1906.

Early medieval vessels fared slightly better. Indeed, north of the Alps, the most common early medieval artifacts are humble items for everyday use that were buried in the graves of their former owners and were recovered by chance or through archeological excavations. These artifacts, although valued as information about their owners by scholars in the countries where they were found, attracted little attention in North America before 1911–1912, when J. Pierpont Morgan lent to the Metropolitan Museum more than 1,000 early medieval objects, including glass vessels, found in France and Germany. A few other institutions, notably the Royal Ontario Museum in Toronto, Canada, and The Cleveland Museum of Art, also acquired early medieval artifacts (mostly metal objects), but the widespread perception remained that the early Middle Ages were, in cultural terms, a chasm that somehow separated the civilizations of ancient Rome and late medieval and Renaissance Europe (Effros 2005). One of the aims of *Medieval Glass for Popes, Princes, and Peasants* is to show that, in the field of glassmaking, far from being a chasm, the Middle Ages were a vital but underappreciated bridge between those peaks of European achievement.

MEDIEVAL GLASS VESSELS: AN OUTLINE

The following paragraphs provide an overview of the varieties of glass described, one by one, in the catalog on pages 88–255. The first section of the catalog (entries **1**–**6**) contains a selection of late Roman glass that shows the range and technical expertise of the Roman glassworker. This is followed by a group of drinking vessels (**7**–**16**) made between the fifth and eighth centuries, and recovered from pagan cemeteries in Germany, the Low Countries, northern France, and England. **17** and **18** belong in part to the Viking Age and were found in Scandinavia.

The largest groups of objects were made in the late Middle Ages. Nearly all of these glasses are bottles and beakers that were intended for use at the table and in the tavern. Most of **19**–**62** are made of glass that is colorless or nearly colorless, either because the glassmakers carefully selected raw materials of unusual purity or because they added a small quantity of manganese oxide, which counteracts impurities such as iron that color the glass green or brown (depending on conditions in the furnace). **63**–**110** are mostly transparent green *Waldglas* (forest glass) made in Germany and the Low Countries.

The next two sections of the catalog illustrate particular themes: the use of glass as liturgical vessels, lighting devices, and reliquaries in churches and other sacred spaces (**104** and **113**–**117**), and the use of glass for scientific and medical purposes (**118**–**120**). Both sections include objects from the Islamic world. Finally, **121**–**128** demonstrate the mastery of Venetian glassmaking during the Renaissance, when craftsmen, building on the accomplishments of late medieval glassworkers, produced some of the most stunning vessels in the entire history of glass.

German terms are used to identify the various shapes of German glasses for which there are no equivalents in English-speaking countries. The spellings in this book are modern German.

Glassmaking in Ancient Rome:
The End of a Tradition

Prologue

IN THE FOURTH and fifth centuries, the Romans' glass-melting technology and their repertoire of techniques for forming and decorating glass were the best in the world. As in earlier times, glassmaking and glassworking often took place in separate locations. Glassmakers melted raw materials to produce glass, while glassworkers formed the glass into finished products. Most glassmakers' workshops were situated near sources of sand, the main ingredient in glass, and of fuel for the furnace.

Roman glassmakers used reverberatory tank furnaces to melt raw materials in larger quantities than ever before. In 1963, a team of archeologists from the University of Missouri in Columbia and The Corning Museum of Glass discovered a huge (somewhat later than the Roman period) slab of glass at Beth She'arim, Israel. The slab, which weighs some 18,000 pounds (about 8,200 kilograms), was the result of an unsuccessful attempt to melt raw materials. If the process had succeeded, it would have provided enough glass to make up to 60,000 small bottles of a type widely used in the Roman Empire to contain inexpensive toilet water. Although the remains of smaller tank furnaces have been found in other parts of the Roman Empire, it appears that furnaces in Egypt and the Levant supplied raw glass to workshops throughout the Roman world (Nenna 2000, passim).

Late Roman glassworkers used a variety of techniques to form molten glass into objects that could be decorated while they were still hot, or cold-worked after they had been annealed (cooled to room temperature). The great majority of vessels were formed by blowing, a technique discovered in the first century B.C., the use of which spread to almost all parts of the Roman Empire in the course of the first century A.D. Glassblowers could produce objects quickly, and inexpensive glass vessels became available for everyday use.

The most frequent methods of decorating objects while the glass was still very hot were applying blobs or trails of molten glass and inflating the as yet unformed bubble of glass in a decorated mold. Both techniques were practiced in late Roman times: 5 is a fourth- or fifth-century pitcher decorated with both blobs and trails, while 6 is a fourth- or fifth-century head flask, the body of which was blown in a mold with two vertical sections (the seams created where the two parts joined are clearly visible behind the subject's ears).

Luxury glass of the Hellenistic period (late fourth to late first centuries B.C.) had included vessels decorated with gold foil. The foil was cut to form the desired pattern and

Figure 1
Detail of medallion (3), showing gold-foil decoration that was
sandwiched between two fused glass disks.

sandwiched between two almost identical vessels, one of which was placed inside the other. The vessels were reheated so that, on cooling, they fused. A similar effect was produced in and after the third century A.D., when glassworkers made both vessels and medallions decorated with gold foil (Fig. 1). Such objects are known generically as gold glasses (*Glass of the Caesars* 1987, pp. 262–268 and 276–286, nos. 152–161).

The medallions were created by sandwiching the foil between two glass disks, which were reheated and fused. Almost all of the vessels, on the other hand, consisted of dishes and bowls formed by blowing and decorated with roundels at the center. The glass that would become the base was blown, and gold foil was applied to the upper surface. After the decoration had been created with a stylus, a bubble of glass was inflated and pressed against the decorated surface. The two layers of glass fused, protecting the gold roundel, and, after softening the glass by reheating, the craftsman worked the vessel into the desired shape. The rims and sides of almost all of the surviving vessels have been completely removed, and only the roundels survive (they include 3 and 4). Roundels were frequently removed from the rest of the vessels and affixed to the walls of catacombs beside burial niches. (Catacombs are subterranean galleries that were used in the early centuries A.D. as Christian and Jewish burial places in Rome and elsewhere.)

The decoration of gold glasses was created before the hot-working of the objects had been completed. Cut and engraved decoration, on the other hand, was added after completion of the forming process. The object was given to a glass cutter or engraver, who decorated it by removing glass with a rotating wheel and/or engraving it with a hand-held tool. We know very little about the tools used for these purposes, although information on the working of semiprecious stones (for example, by Pliny the Elder in the first century A.D.) probably applies equally well to cold-working glass; indeed, it is not unlikely that some of the same craftsmen worked with both materials.

A considerable variety of late Roman cold-worked glass objects exists, and scholars have recognized the products of different regions or workshops. Among the most distinctive products are bottles with wheel-abraded scenes depicting prominent landmarks in the Roman cities of Baiae, a seaside resort in the southern Italian region of Campania, and Puteoli, a port and commercial center, also in Campania (1). Rome itself supported a number of cutting shops, some of which produced vessels depicting the emperor and members of the imperial court (e.g., *Glass of the Caesars* 1987, pp. 223–224, no. 124).

The rarest of all late Roman luxury glasses are objects with "cages" made by grinding and polishing the glass after it had been annealed. The glassworker took a blank with unusually thick sides and removed half to two-thirds of the glass to make a vessel (usually a beaker, bowl, or lamp) enclosed by an openwork cage attached to the wall and base by well-concealed posts. The copper-alloy collar of **2** indicates that the object was probably a hanging lamp. The fastener of the collar is corroded, suggesting that it has been attached to the vessel since Roman times.

The Early and Central Middle Ages

FLAT GLASS and beads apart, the history of glass in the early and central Middle Ages is essentially the history of drinking vessels. Although the great majority of complete early medieval vessels have been recovered from graves, the occurrence of fragments of identical types in settlements shows that the objects buried with the dead were the same as those used by the living. Conversely, much of the glass of the central Middle Ages that is known to us was found at inhabited sites: settlements, monasteries, and palaces. In the following pages, the focus of attention is a region comprising part of Germany, the Low Countries, northern France, and England, although attention is also paid to finds from Scandinavia.

THE EARLY MIDDLE AGES

During this period, the quantity and quality of glass vessels made in Europe declined sharply. Nevertheless, chemical analyses of European vessels show that raw glass made with natron continued to be imported from the eastern Mediterranean through the seventh century, supplemented to an unknown extent by recycled glass recovered from Roman sites, and by tesserae salvaged from Roman ruins to add color to the batch (the mixture of raw materials that is melted to make glass).

The basic forms of the glass vessels used in these areas in the early Middle Ages (fifth to seventh centuries) are:

1. Bowls
2. Cups
3. Beakers
4. Drinking horns
5. Bottles

1. Bowls

The earliest bowls of the Migration Period resemble Roman bowls made in the Rhineland and elsewhere in the fourth and fifth centuries. They are mostly shallow and have a cracked-off rim. (Cracking off is the mechanical process of detaching the unwanted part of a mass of glass on

Tavern scene with men drinking from bottles and beakers, with a cellarer below. Detail from illustration shown on page 17.

the end of a blowpipe, which leaves a rough rim that is often smoothed by grinding.) The sides of the bowls may be straight or curved, and the base is either flat or rounded. Some bowls have vertical indentations in the wall; other types of decoration include dip-molded ribs, sometimes in a spiral pattern, and trailing. The trailed decoration may consist of spirally wound threads that give the appearance of being parallel horizontal lines, and arcades. Some of the trails were left in low relief, while others were marvered until they were flush with the wall.

Later bowls, like almost all other early medieval vessels, have rounded rims made by reheating the mouth of the vessel until it became soft, and fire polishing removed the irregularities that characterize cracked-off rims.

2. Cups

The most frequent form of cup is a small hemispherical or bell-shaped vessel that would fit in the palm of one's hand: hence the name "palm cup." Palm cups may have a plain, fire-polished rim or a rim that was folded out and down to produce the appearance of a collar. As with most other varieties of early medieval drinking vessels, cups may be undecorated or have dip-molded ribs or trails.

3. Beakers

Most early medieval beakers are of three basic types: cone beakers, bell beakers, and claw beakers.

Cone beakers, as their name implies, are glasses with a plain or slightly everted rim, a straight and tapering side, and a narrow flat or rounded base. The base is so small that the beakers cannot stand, and we assume that the contents were intended to be drained by one or more drinkers and that, when not in use, the vessels were stored upside down. Some cone beakers have straight or spiraling ribs made by blowing the bubble of molten glass into a decorated mold, while others have trailed decoration, which may or may not have been marvered until the trails were flush with the vessel wall. **9** is an elegant example of a cone beaker with trailed decoration, and **10**, which was found in a cemetery at Faversham, Kent, in southeastern England, is unusual among early medieval glasses from the British Isles in that it is believed to have been made locally rather than imported from the Continent.

Bell beakers, again as the name implies, resemble inverted bells with a flaring rim, a side with a more or less S-shaped profile, and a pointed base that sometimes terminates in a knob. Like the cone beakers, bell beakers cannot stand, and presumably they rested on their rims. Bell beakers are sometimes decorated with ribs formed in a dip mold, and a small group of vessels (including **8**), mainly from the Aube region of northeastern France, have mold-blown inscriptions. Other bell beakers are decorated with "horizontal" trails (in fact, trails wound in tight spirals around the wall) or with trailed arcades in a continuous band around the lower wall.

The claw beaker originated in the fourth century, when glassmakers in Cologne, Germany, and probably in other parts of the Rhineland, Belgium, and northern France began to make extensive use of three-dimensional "claws" or "trunks" to decorate the walls of cups, beakers, and bowls (Follman-Schulz 1995). Each claw was made by applying a blob of molten glass to the side of the vessel while it was still on the blowpipe. The side became soft at the point of contact, and a combination of inflation and pulling the blob out and down resulted in the creation of a hollow clawlike projection, which could be embellished by the addition and manipulation of bits and trails of hot glass (see page 113). One such vessel, of very pale green glass, decorated with claws that resemble dolphins with bright blue jaws and fins, was found in Cologne and is attributed to the second half of the fourth century (*Glass of the Caesars* 1987, p. 256, no. 145). Among the earliest true claw beakers are a vessel from a mid-fifth-century grave at Krefeld-Gellep, between Bonn and Cologne, and a similar object—evidently an heirloom at the time of its burial—from a sixth-century grave at Mucking in southeastern England (*ibid.*, pp. 257–258, no. 146).

4. Drinking Horns

Drinking vessels shaped like the horns of cattle and similar animals have been used in many cultures. They may be real animal horns or imitations made of metal, earthenware, or glass. In Europe, the Romans used glass drinking horns in two periods: the first century A.D. and the third to fifth centuries. First-century drinking horns, which often stood on a hollow foot, had a small aperture at the tip, through which the liquid was poured into the drinker's mouth (Whitehouse 1997, pp. 118–120, nos. 184–186). Later Roman drinking horns, which may have been a German specialty, had neither a stand nor a hole at the tip; users drank by upending them. One example, from a fourth-century burial in Cologne, had two loops to receive a strap for suspension (*Glass of the Caesars* 1987, p. 117, no. 49), and similar suspension loops appear on a glass horn found at Trier (Goethert-Polaschek 1977, p. 260, no. 1542).

The use of drinking horns continued in the early Middle Ages, although examples made of glass were never common (Evison 1975). Among the finds from the Continent are two fifth-century glass horns, decorated with marvered trails, that were found in cemeteries at Krefeld-Gellep and Mézières, Ardennes, France (Cabart and Feyeux 1995, p. 107, no. 297). A pair of horns embellished with thick, unmarvered trails was excavated from a late sixth- to seventh-century grave at Rainham, Essex, in southeastern England (Evison 2008, p. 52, nos. 47 and 48).

5. Bottles

Early medieval bottles, which are common in the Rhineland and northeastern France but rare in England, are of two types. The first type is small and has a short funnel-shaped rim, a narrow neck, a roughly globular body, and a flat base. **15** is an example of a small bottle that seems to have been used as a reliquary, since it bears an engraved inscription that refers to the shrine of Saint Ursula and the 11,000 Virgins at Cologne, Germany.

The second, somewhat larger type of bottle also has a short funnel-shaped rim and a narrow neck, but the body is more or less cylindrical. The wall may have a slight bulge at the bottom, and the base usually has a low kick (an indentation on the underside, with a corresponding convex or conical protrusion on the vessel's interior), which is much less pronounced than the tall, conical kicks in the bases of many late medieval vessels (see pages 73–76). **16** is a late Roman or early medieval cylindrical bottle without a bulge at the bottom of the wall.

Changes in the repertoire of the early medieval glass vessels used in Germany, the Low Countries, northern France, and England may be divided into two stages: (1) from about 400 to 550 and (2) from 550 to 700. Bowls were present in both stages; many of the earlier examples have cracked-off rims, while the rims of later specimens are fire-polished. Among the beakers, cone beakers were made in both stages, as were bell beakers. The same is true of claw beakers, but, unlike the other types, they continued to be made in the eighth century. Bottles were made in stages 1 and 2, but palm cups and glass drinking horns were either unknown or little known in stage 1; they were current in stage 2, and their production continued into the eighth century.

THE CENTRAL MIDDLE AGES

The following pages contain a brief survey of glass vessels made between the eighth and 11th centuries.

When Christianity became the most widely accepted religion in central and western Europe, the custom of burying objects in graves ceased (except in pagan Scandinavia) and our sources of information about the production and use of glass changed. Instead of studying complete objects and associated artifacts deposited in graves, archeologists work with fragmentary vessels from the sites of settlements, monasteries, and forts. Despite the incomplete nature of almost all of this evidence, there is a clear impression that glassmakers then had access to a greater range of techniques (and a larger number of wealthy customers) than at any time since the fifth century.

Vessel glass of the Carolingian and Ottonian periods has been recovered from four main kinds of archeological sites: emporiums (trading centers and ports of entry); palaces and other elite residences, such as Charlemagne's palace at Paderborn, Germany; churches and monasteries, such as San Vincenzo al Volturno, Italy; and, less frequently, glassmakers' workshops, some of which have been found in emporiums, palaces, and monasteries.

The number of shapes of the glass of the Carolingian and Ottonian periods (which collectively occupied most of the time between 750 and 1024) appears to be limited, although the fragmentary nature of most finds may prevent us from recognizing the full range of shapes and decoration. The known forms include funnel beakers (some of which may have been lamps for suspension in polycandela: see page 53), globular beakers or jars, dishes, and bottles.

Figure 1
Funnel beaker. Illustration of the month of November from a 10th-century manuscript of the Martyrology of Saint Wandalbert (d. about 870). Biblioteca Apostolica Vaticana (Ms. Reg. Lat. 438).

The decoration, on the other hand, is rather varied. It includes ribs formed by blowing in dip molds, overall patterns resembling bunches of grapes blown in molds with two parts, applied monochrome and *reticello* canes (that is, canes composed of twisted colorless and white or yellow threads, which were reheated and applied to the surface of the vessel), and unprotected gold foil. Vessels shaped like bunches of grapes, *reticello* canes, and decoration with gold foil all have Roman antecedents (cf. *Glass of the Caesars* 1987, p. 170, no. 91, p. 39, no. 15, and p. 273, no. 150 respectively), but there is no reason to believe that they were made continuously throughout the early centuries A.D.

The most complete or almost complete examples of these types have been found in pagan cemeteries associated with Viking ship burials and emporiums in Scandinavia and north-western Germany. Funnel beakers (similar to **17**; Fig. 1), for example, have been excavated from a ninth-century woman's grave at Birka, Sweden, and from a ninth- to 10th-century ship burial at Haithabu, Germany. Beakers shaped like a bunch of grapes (*Traubenbecher*) were discovered in a ninth-century grave (539) at Birka and a ninth- to 10th-century context at Haithabu. Fragments of a deep blue vessel decorated with opaque white trails came from a deposit of the first half of the 11th century at Birka. Glasses decorated with *reticello* trails were found in Ship Burial 6 at Valsgaarde, Sweden, which is usually dated to about 750, and in Grave 649 at Birka, which dates from the ninth to 10th centuries. Fragments of colorless or strongly colored vessels with gold-foil ornament have been recovered from Helgö, Sweden, and the North Sea emporium at Dorestad, the Netherlands (for all of these finds, see *Phönix aus Sand und Asche* 1988, pp. 58–84).

In spite of its distance from Scandinavia, the Benedictine monastery of San Vincenzo al Volturno in the Molise region of southern Italy provides numerous parallels for some of the glasses described above (Stevenson 2001), suggesting that similar objects were widely available. It is not surprising, however, given the location of San Vincenzo, that the fragmentary eighth- and ninth-century glass vessels include both types that were developed in the Mediterranean region and types that are found farther north. Among the former are truncated conical lamps with two or three vertical handles attached to the rim, and goblets with a bowl shaped like half an egg, a solid stem, and a hollow conical foot made by folding. Another form that originated in the Mediterranean region, but subsequently was adopted all over Europe, is a lamp with an open, cup-shaped reservoir and a hollow tubular stem, similar to **104**.

Glass that has parallels north of the Alps includes fragments decorated with *reticello* canes and opaque yellow and opaque white trails. Some of this material was recovered from the remains of an early ninth-century glassmaker's workshop, but it is not clear whether such objects were made there or whether they were made elsewhere and were taken to the workshop for recycling. Another example of a medieval vessel with *reticello* decoration, perhaps found in Italy, is an intact palm cup in the Antiquarium Romanum in the Musei Vaticani (Fremersdorf 1975, p. 94, no. 860).

Despite the recovery of a limited number of complete or almost complete vessels from graves in Scandinavia, much of our knowledge of the domestic glass of the eighth and ninth centuries in northern and western Europe has been gleaned from excavations at the sites of emporiums, the trading settlements that grew up around the shores of the North and Baltic Seas. Excavations at Dorestad, located at the junction of the Rhine and Lek Rivers in the Netherlands, provided an important sample (Isings 1980), but an even larger group of vessel glass was recovered during long-term excavations at Hamwic, the Saxon forerunner of Southampton, a major port on the English Channel, which was occupied between the early eighth and early ninth centuries (Hunter and Heyworth 1998).

The excavation at Hamwic produced more than 1,700 fragments of vessel glass—one of the largest collections of glass of this period from a single site anywhere in Europe. However, the fragments are very small, and it is not clear how many of them arrived as fragments, perhaps to be recycled for beadmaking, and how many arrived as complete vessels intended for use. To judge by the shapes and diameters of the rim fragments, many of the vessels were palm cups and beakers, usually of transparent pale blue or green glass, and in many cases with light ribbing formed by inflating the bubble of glass in a dip mold. In addition to mold-blown decoration, the fragments included glass with opaque yellow or opaque white marvered trails, and *reticello* canes. The collection also includes fragments of red, blue, and purple glass. Overall, the quality of the assemblage, like the vessels from Scandinavia and San Vincenzo al Volturno, represents "a high point in post-Roman glass [reflecting] levels of craftsmanship and technology unequalled until the [late] Middle Ages" (*ibid.*, p. 61).

In the course of the eighth century, European glassmakers had begun to produce their own raw glass, using wood ash as the alkaline flux; chemical analyses show that glass made with wood ash was in use in Charlemagne's palace in Paderborn, Germany, before about 780 (see page 66).

After the eighth century, the use of beech ash was standard in most parts of Europe. One, presumably unsuspected, by-product of its use was a lowering of the temperature at which the raw materials melted. The earliest recipe that describes this low-temperature batch is in a compendium titled "De diversis artibus" (On various arts), attributed to Theophilus and written between about 1110 and 1140. "De diversis artibus" is an often detailed account of crafts practiced in the early 12th century, from ivory carving and wall painting to manuscript illumination and glassmaking. (Incidentally, it includes the first European reference to paper.) "Theophilus" was probably the pseudonym of Roger of Helmarshausen, who made a portable altar that is now in the treasury of the cathedral in Paderborn. Theophilus describes how to make glasses of different colors, including glass colored with lead, and gilded glass made "by Greeks" (see **111**). Figure 2 is an 11th-century illustration of a glass furnace, which either represents a furnace used in the central Middle Ages or was copied from an earlier manuscript.

Figure 2
Glassblower and furnace. From a manuscript of Rabanus Maurus, "De universo"
(On the universe) (1023). Montecassino Abbey (Ms. 132, f.427).

The Late Middle Ages

AS THE ECONOMY expanded, glassmakers increased the quantity and variety of their products. In this chapter, we consider a selection of glass vessels made between the late 12th and early 16th centuries. They are divided into four groups: (1) vessels for domestic use; (2) a "Hedwig beaker," one of a group of objects that seem to have been used in both domestic and religious contexts; (3) vessels used in sacred spaces; and (4) vessels used for scientific and medical purposes. Although most of the objects were made in Germany and adjoining countries, a small number of exotic glasses were made in the Mediterranean region and imported as luxurious items for use or display.

In the southern part of the area that concerns us—southern Germany, Switzerland, and northern and central Italy—the best late medieval glass was either colorless or almost colorless but with a yellowish tinge. In northern and central Europe, on the other hand, most locally produced glass was transparent green *Waldglas* (forest glass), so called because it was made in small factories situated in forested areas where fuel was immediately available. The colorless glass was produced by carefully selecting the raw materials and by adding a small quantity of manganese oxide. As in the case of many earlier glasses, the green color of the forest glass was caused by iron oxide and other impurities in the raw materials.

VESSELS FOR DOMESTIC USE

The word *domestic* is applied here to the homes of almost all social classes, from the relatively poor to the very rich. Many of the glasses described here would have been used at the table (as numerous late medieval paintings attest), although they could equally well have served elsewhere in the home.

Glass for Daily Use: Late 12th to 14th Centuries

Finds from archeological excavations indicate that the great majority of late 12th- to 14th-century glass vessels used at home were intended for serving and consuming liquid. Late medieval paintings of the Last Supper (Fig. 1), the Wedding at Cana (Fig. 2), and Herod's Feast depict tables set with one or more bottles and a larger number of beakers or goblets,

Shops and a market in Siena, Italy, as shown in Ambrogio Lorenzetti's *The Effects of Good Government* (1338–1340), a fresco in the Palazzo Pubblico, Siena.

Figure 1
Magdalen Master, *The Last Supper*, late 13th century. Musée du Petit Palais, Avignon.

although not enough for everyone to have his or her own vessel; evidently, glasses were shared, as indeed were knives and other utensils.

The following paragraphs contain descriptions of these forms in the following order: beakers (vessels with straight, usually tapering sides, similar to modern tumblers), goblets (vessels with a bowl, stem, and foot), and bottles.

Apart from the vessels of the "Aldrevandin" group (described on pages 41–42), beakers from this period are plain, were decorated by inflating the molten glass in a mold, or have applied ornament. Most undecorated beakers are small, and the diameter of the rim is frequently greater than the height. They have a plain, fire-polished rim and a base with a conical kick, the purpose of which is discussed on pages 73–76. The beakers with mold-blown decoration are usually of similar proportions. The decoration covers the wall from the rim or just below the rim to the base. It consists of an overall pattern of a single small motif (Fig. 3). The exceptionally large sample of glass from late 14th-century deposits in the Palazzo Vitelleschi at Tarquinia, in central Italy, included fragments of 270 beakers with mold-blown decoration,

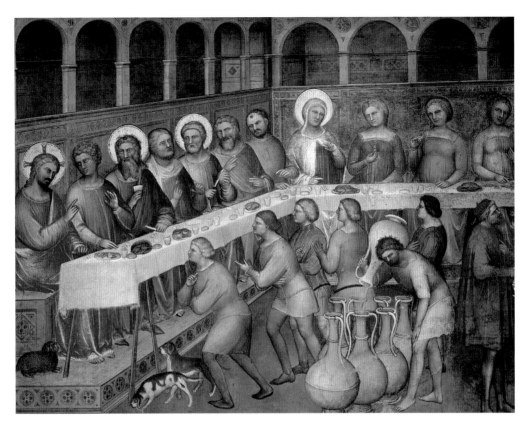

Figure 2
Giusto de' Menabuoi, *The Wedding at Cana* (1378). Fresco in the baptistery of Padua Cathedral. The table is set with various mold-blown and prunted beakers.

Figure 3
Detail from *The Wedding at Cana* (above), showing a beaker with mold-blown decoration.

of which 137 (51%) have small circular bosses, 91 (34%) have vertical ribs, and 27 (10%) have a honeycomb pattern of adjoining hexagons (Newby 1999, v. 1, p. 57).

The beakers with applied decoration come in a variety of shapes and sizes, usually with the height greater than the diameter of the rim. The smaller vessels may have a roughly barrel-shaped body and a short rim, which may be vertical or slightly tapered, while the larger examples may have tapering sides and a tall, tapering rim. A trail forms a continuous horizontal rib at the junction of the rim and the wall. Another trail was wound once around the junction of the wall and the base, and this was either left plain or tooled to form a row of small projecting "toes." The area between these trails was filled with ornament (Figs. 4 and 5).

Figure 4
Prunted beaker. Detail from the Codex
Manesse, a collection of songs compiled
between about 1300 and 1340, probably
for the patrician Manesse family of
Zurich. Heidelberg University Library
(Cod. Pal. Germ. 848, f.80).

Figure 5
Prunted beakers. Detail from Giusto de' Menabuoi,
The Wedding at Cana (Figure 2).

The ornament falls into several distinct types. The most common type consists of horizontal rows of prunts: small blobs of glass applied to the wall, the centers of which were pulled into the shape of a nipple (e.g., **22**). Depending on the size of the vessel, there are from two to 11 rows of prunts; in each row, the prunts are placed above or below the gaps between the prunts in the next row (e.g., **23**). A second type of applied decoration comprises several horizontal trails, in which almost colorless glass may alternate with deep blue glass and plain trails may alternate with trails that have been pinched to form rows of short vertical ridges. Vertical ribs represent a third type of applied ornament.

Goblets, unlike beakers, consist of three elements: a bowl, a stem, and a foot (Fig. 6). For many years, the goblet was thought to be a drinking vessel exclusive to the Renaissance and later, which replaced the ubiquitous late medieval beaker. We know now that this was not the case. Goblets are found in 13th- and 14th-century archeological contexts in many parts of Europe: *Phönix aus Sand und Asche* (1988) contained some 60 examples, mainly from Germany and northeastern France; *A travers le verre* (1989) offered more than 30 examples

Figure 6
Three goblets. A banquet at the king's court, from the historiated Bible of Guyart
des Moulins and Pierre Comestor (late 13th to early 14th centuries). Bibliothèque
Universitaire de Médecine, Montpellier (H 49, F.239v).

from France; others have been published from sites in central Europe and Italy; and Tyson (2000, pp. 50–70) published finds from England, most if not all of which were imported from the Continent. Several varieties of decoration are found: many French goblets have mold-blown bowls with prominent vertical ribs, which project below the wall at its junction with the base, while others have lightly molded geometric patterns covering the lower wall and the base. Applied decoration may include trails on the bowl and openwork embellishments on the stem.

Most bottles fall into one of two groups: those that were free-blown and those that were blown into a ribbed dip mold, withdrawn, and inflated further to obtain the desired shape and size. Such bottles commonly have a narrow neck and a globular or onion-shaped body (Fig. 7), usually with a tall conical kick and sometimes with a trumpet-shaped foot (Fig. 8). There are numerous

Figure 7
Ewer and bottle. Detail from Taddeo Gaddi, painting (about 1330) in the Baroncelli Chapel in Santa Croce, Florence.

Figure 8
Two bottles and a beaker. Detail
from Domenico Ghirlandaio,
fresco depicting the birth of John
the Baptist (1494). Santa Maria
Novella, Florence.

variants. The neck may have a bulge a short distance below the rim (Fig. 9), and the body
may have an internal tubular ring, made by folding, at the greatest diameter. Presumably this
latter feature was intended to strengthen the vessel, which typically has very thin walls.

This distinctive repertoire of beakers with mold-blown or applied decoration, goblets,
and bottles has no obvious antecedents in western Europe, and so it is understandable that
students of medieval glass sought its origin elsewhere. Consequently, for half a century, opin-
ions about its origin and early development were based largely on similar but apparently
earlier finds from a single archeological site: Corinth.

In 1937, the remains of two medieval glassmakers' workshops were discovered in the agora
(the former marketplace) of Corinth, one of the great Greco-Roman cities of southern
Greece. The excavators named these workshops Agora Northeast and Agora South Center.
The workshops were thought to be of the same date, although the glassworkers used different
manufacturing processes and made different products. For us, the focus of attention is the
Agora South Center workshop.

The excavation of the Agora South Center workshop revealed large quantities of broken
glass vessels: beakers with mold-blown and applied decoration, goblets, and bottles of various
shapes and sizes. The excavators concluded that the workshop was active in the 11th and
early 12th centuries, a conclusion supported by the discovery of numerous coins apparently
struck during the reign of Emperor Manuel I (1143–1180). The finds, therefore, were believed
to represent the repertoire of Middle Byzantine glassmakers in Greece (Davidson 1952, pp.
83–122).

The glass from Corinth resembles glass vessels from sites in Italy and adjoining regions,
and scholars sought an explanation for the occurrence of similar objects in Greece and Italy.
The exploits of a fleet from Norman Sicily, which raided southern Greece in 1147, appeared to

Figure 9
Four beakers and two bottles. Detail of the Gluttons, from a fresco
of the Inferno by Taddeo di Bartolo (1393) in the Cathedral of San Gimignano.

provide a link. The chronicler Nicetas Choniates (about 1140–1213) recorded that the Normans transported silk workers from the Greek city of Thebes to Palermo, Sicily, together with prominent citizens from Corinth. If the Normans also captured glassworkers, it was argued, this might explain the demise of the Agora South Center workshop. Moreover, glassworkers from Greece could have introduced the Byzantine glass industry to Sicily, whence it could have spread to the mainland of Italy and other parts of western Europe (*ibid.*, pp. 83 and 88).

The similarities between late medieval glass from Corinth and from Italy, Switzerland, and parts of Germany became increasingly apparent as excavations added more and more examples from western Europe. At the same time, the new archeological discoveries revealed a disparity between the supposed date of the glass from Corinth (11th to 12th centuries) and the date of similar objects farther west (13th to 14th centuries).

Four pieces of evidence compelled glass historians to reinterpret the chronology of the Agora South Center workshop and the origin of the glass found there. First, a close reading of reports on the discovery of the workshop suggests that finds from nearly one meter of superimposed deposits, some of which were earlier than the workshop itself, may have been combined. This means that we cannot determine from the published accounts which coins and glass came from the workshop and which were from earlier deposits, with the result that the excavation reports tell us little about the date of the workshop (Whitehouse 1991, p. 77; Williams 2003).

The second piece of evidence was revealed in the publication of the structural history of the South Center area in medieval times: "Throughout the entire area the buildings of the twelfth century survived in considerable parts through the thirteenth century at least, subject to repair and remodeling (Scranton 1957, p. 86; see also Williams 2003).

Third, as the Italian scholar Astone Gasparetto (1975, p. 145) remarked, according to Choniates, the only artisans transported to Palermo were the Theban weavers. There is, therefore, no documentary evidence for the removal of glassmakers from Corinth in 1147.

The final, decisive evidence consisted of finds from Corinth in the early 1990s, when the same repertoire of glass vessels associated with the Agora South Center workshop was recovered from contexts securely dated to the "last twenty-five years before the Catalan invasion of 1312." Moreover, numerous coins of Manuel I, identical to those used to date the workshop, were shown to be later imitations, and at the time of the Catalan invasion, Corinth was in the hands of Italians (Williams and Zervos 1993, p. 15; Williams and Zervos 1995; Williams 2003).

In short, the archeological evidence for attributing the workshop to the 11th and early 12th centuries was unsound, and the historical evidence for the transportation of Corinthian glassmakers to Sicily in 1147 is nonexistent. In any case, we know now that glassware identical to the products of the workshop is typical of that used in late 13th- and early 14th-century Corinth.

All things considered, it is now believed that the Agora South Center workshop, far from being an 11th- to early 12th-century Byzantine factory producing glass that inspired imitations in western Europe, was a 13th-century workshop operated by Italians.

Aldrevandin Glasses

Aldrevandin glasses take their name from a beaker in The British Museum (Fig. 10) that came to public attention in 1876, when it was displayed in an exhibition in Munich, Germany. The catalog of that exhibition provides a partial identification of the three coats of arms that adorn the beaker: (1) perhaps the Nellenburg family, (2) the Portners of Augsburg or the Schützens of Franconia, and (3) the von Liebersteins of Swabia. The coats of arms were compared with those depicted in the "Wappenrolle von Zürich," an illustrated catalog of coats of arms compiled in Zurich, Switzerland, in the 1320s. In fact, the three stags' antlers and their color scheme correspond exactly to the arms of the Nellenburgs in the early 14th century. Just below the rim of the beaker is a Latin inscription: "MAGISTER ALDREVAN-DIN ME FECI" (Master Aldrevandin made me)—hence its name.

Almost immediately after the exhibition closed, The British Museum acquired the beaker. According to the museum's director, forgeries of the object were on the market in 1902, although only one of these, the Hope Goblet, has been recognized, and its date is uncertain (Freestone, Gudenrath, and Cartwright 2008; Krueger 2008).

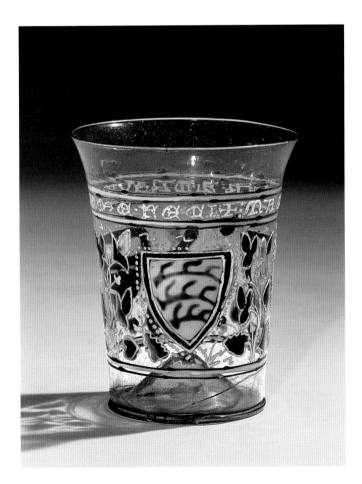

Figure 10
The Aldrevandin Beaker, blown, with polychrome enameled decoration applied to both the outer and inner surfaces. Venice, late 13th century. H. 13 cm. The British Museum, London (76.11-4.3).

In her classic study of the Aldrevandin glasses, Ingeborg Krueger (2002) surveyed the enameled glasses that the maker of the Hope Goblet may have examined and imitated. The Historisches Museum Basel in Switzerland had preserved fragments of a bowl since 1870; a beaker, now in Frankfurt am Main, Germany, was well known, as perhaps was a beaker acquired by the Landesmuseum Württemberg, Stuttgart, also in Germany, in 1916. Archeological finds included fragments of a beaker from Restormel Castle, United Kingdom, and fragments in the Bayerisches Nationalmuseum, Munich.

The idea that the Aldrevandin glasses form a coherent group that combines Western iconography with the Islamic technique of enameling on glass and so originated in the Crusader states of the Levant became orthodox in the early 20th century. Edward Dillon (1907, p. 176) described them as "Venetian or Franco-Syrian." Later, Robert Schmidt (1922, pp. 56–58) and Carl Johan Lamm (1929–30, pp. 246 and 278–285) defined the group as "Syro-Frankish" and noted that if the glasses originated in the Levant, they should be earlier than 1291, when the last significant Crusader possession, Acre, fell to the Mamluks.

However, in the late 1960s and the 1970s, Luigi Zecchin published archival evidence from Venice that showed the local presence of painters of glass vessels in the late 13th and early 14th centuries. Indeed, Zecchin calculated that, in 1287, a painter named Gregorio produced no fewer than 4,400 enameled beakers (Carboni 1998, pp. 102 and 105, n. 24)! Consequently, Venice re-emerged as the only known place in Europe where the Aldrevandin glasses could have been made. As with so many aspects of medieval glass studies, the exhibition and catalog *Phönix aus Sand und Asche* (1988) summed up what was then known about the objects: examples had been found in archeological excavations in several parts of Europe; when they came from datable contexts, they were of the same period as the Venetian documents; and, although Venice may not have been the only place of manufacture, it was almost certainly one of them.

In the two decades since the publication of *Phönix aus Sand und Asche*, many more finds have come to light, from Italy to Scandinavia and the British Isles. Indeed, the quantity of finds shows that Aldrevandin glasses were not rare objects made for elite customers, but were produced for a larger public—as Zecchin's calculation indicated. In addition to Aldrevandin (or Aldrevandinus), examples bear the names of other painters: Doninus, Petrus, and Bartolomeus. Although a Venetian document describes a certain Doninus as "pictor muzolorum de vitro de Muriano" (a painter of glass beakers from Murano), the large number of finds from Germany may suggest that some Aldrevandin vessels were made north of the Alps.

Forest Glass: 15th to Early 16th Centuries

Most of the glass vessels produced in the later Middle Ages in northern Germany, the Low Countries, and central Europe were made of transparent green *Waldglas* (forest glass). They were produced in small glasshouses located in forests (Fig. 11), which provided a ready source of fuel, and their color was caused by the presence of impurities, principally iron oxide, in

Figure 11
Forest glass workshop. From a manuscript of the travels of Sir John
Mandeville, probably produced in Bohemia (about 1410). The British
Library, London (Ms. Add. 24189, f.16).

Figure 12
Beaker with mold-blown ribs. Detail
from Justus of Ghent, triptych of the
Crucifixion (about 1465). Saint Bavo's
Cathedral, Ghent.

the raw materials, especially the sand. The repertoire of forest glass, although varied, consists
mainly of vessels for drinking: mold-blown and prunted beakers, *Stangengläser*, and bottles
for pouring or storing small quantities of liquid.

The most common beakers were direct descendants of earlier medieval forms. Some, for
example, have a truncated conical shape with a plain rim, a straight tapering side, and a base
with a high kick. Many such objects were decorated by blowing the bubble of molten glass
into a dip mold. Some of these beakers have vertical or slanting ribs or overall honeycomb
patterns (Fig. 12 and **64**). Others have more complex patterns that were created by inflating
the bubble in the mold twice, to produce a crisscross effect (**65**). An interesting elaboration
of this dip-molded decoration was made by inserting, into the mouth of the still soft vessel, a
tool with vertical "fins," which resulted in a polygonal rather than circular mouth (**68** and **69**).

One of the descendants of the prunted beaker was a vessel known as the *Krautstrunk*
(cabbage stalk). The name is appropriate: unlike earlier prunts, the applied ornament consisted of large prunts, sometimes with small points, that projected from the green wall of the
vessel like the scars on a cabbage stalk after the leaves have been removed. Among the first
Krautstrünke were barrel-shaped beakers reminiscent of earlier medieval vessels (**43**). Later
glassmakers produced a number of diversified forms, from wide, shallow vessels (**82** and **83**)
to egg-shaped beakers (**74–81**), all of which have large, shallow prunts.

The *Berkemeyer* was another type of drinking vessel derived from late medieval prunted
beakers. It was popular in the 16th and 17th centuries, and it is found chiefly in Germany and
the Low Countries. *Berkemeyer* have a large funnel-shaped mouth and a relatively small body
decorated with prunts (**84**). In addition, some examples have decoration in low relief made

by inflating the bubble of glass in a dip mold (**85**). Occasionally, a *Berkemeyer* stands on a short stem and an openwork foot (**107**).

An entirely different form of drinking vessel, the *Scheuer*, was made in Germany, both in forest glass and in colorless and deliberately colored glasses. *Scheuern* have a short cylindrical neck, a broad biconical or roughly globular body, and a foot (**42**). The foot may be shaped like a disk, splay below a short stem (**88**), or resemble a hollow cone. *Scheuern* made of strongly colored glass include examples of deep green (**88**) and sealing wax red (**109**). The most elaborate vessels have gilded and enameled decoration.

Among the bottles produced in forest glass in and after the 15th century, two distinctive shapes stand out: the biconical bottle and the *Kuttrolf* or *Angster*. Biconical bottles (**97–99**) have a rounded lip and a short neck. The upper part of the body splays to the midpoint, where it expands to form a broad flange, below which the lower wall tapers and merges with a disklike foot. Most bottles of this type are found in Germany and Bohemia, with only rare examples in eastern France (e.g., *A travers le verre* 1989, p. 327, no. 367). Biconical bottles are depicted in a number of 15th- and 16th-century paintings, such as the miniature of a glassblower at his furnace in a manuscript of Rabanus Maurus's "De universo," created in 1425 for Count Palatine Ludwig's library in Heidelberg; a Virgin and Child painted by an unknown artist about 1433 and now in the National Gallery of Victoria in Melbourne, Australia; and a 16th-century painting of a woman playing the clavichord in the Worcester Art Museum in Worcester, Massachusetts (Henkes 1994, p. 49; *Amendt Collection* 2005, pp. 44 and 46).

The *Kuttrolf* or *Angster* is a vessel with a funnel-shaped mouth, a narrow neck, and a globular or hemispherical body (**101–103**). The neck, which was pinched during the forming process, is divided into two or more vertical tubes. Similar objects were made in Germany and adjoining regions during the Roman period, but we have no reason to believe that they were produced continuously thereafter. Instead, the form was reintroduced in the 14th or 15th century. It continued to be popular after the Middle Ages, and Venetian and *façon de Venise* examples were made until the 17th century or even the early 18th century.

In modern literature on the history of glass, the bottle with a divided neck is usually identified as a *Kuttrolf*, and the name is explained as an onomatopoeic reference to the gurgling sound that liquid supposedly makes when it is poured through the narrow tubes. The alternative name, *Angster*, which is probably derived from the Latin adjective *angustus* (narrow), refers to the small diameter of the tubes.

Exotic Glasses for Use and Display

From time to time, exotic glass objects found their way to western and central Europe from the Islamic world and Byzantium. Although the presence of such luxurious objects is sometimes explained in terms of crusaders or pilgrims returning from the Holy Land, it is perhaps more likely that the majority arrived as items of trade or gifts. Some of these prestigious glasses have survived as prized possessions and heirlooms of princely families; others (a growing number), however, are finds from archeological excavations, mainly on urban sites, indicating that merchant families as well as aristocrats occasionally had access to exotic glassware from distant countries.

Byzantine Gilded and Enameled Glass

In the early 12th century, a German monk known as Theophilus (probably a pseudonym) compiled a treatise titled "De diversis artibus" (On various arts), in which he noted that Greeks gilded blue glass drinking vessels in two ways: by applying the gold as foil and by mixing gold dust with a liquid and applying it as paint. Theophilus's description of decorating with gold foil is difficult to understand, but his account of liquid gilding, although it contains mistakes, is clear enough: "With it they make circles and, in them, animals or birds. . . . Then they take white, red, and green glass, which are used for enamels, and carefully grind each one. . . . With them, they paint small flowers and scrolls and other small things they want, in varied work, between the circles and scrolls, and a border around the rim" (2.14: Theophilus 1961, pp. 45–46).

This is an accurate description of a group of vessels from sites in the eastern Mediterranean, notably Paphos on Cyprus and Corinth in Greece (**111**: Whitehouse 1998, 2002). Other examples have been found in Italy, the British Isles, Sweden, and elsewhere, and it is entirely possible that Theophilus, even if he never left Germany, had seen one; his description certainly implies firsthand knowledge.

The most common forms are narrow cylindrical beakers and cylindrical bottles with a short neck and narrow mouth. The decoration is arranged in horizontal rows of roundels containing birds or animals, or in horizontal panels containing animals or human figures. One of the characteristic features of the gilding is the use of scratches to indicate details. Another common feature is the presence of spiraling arabesques.

Finds of beakers and bottles at Saranda Kolones, the site of a castle near Paphos, show that they were in use sometime between 1191 (when the castle was built) and 1222 (when it was destroyed by an earthquake). Thus, if these glasses are indeed the vessels described by Theophilus, they were in use for a large part of the 12th century.

Islamic Gilded and Enameled Glass

The most spectacular glass made in the Islamic world in the Middle Ages was decorated with gilding and vitreous enamel. Between the late 12th and early 15th centuries, in regions mostly ruled by the Ayyubid and Mamluk dynasties (regions that extended from present-day Syria to Egypt), glass workshops produced large numbers of objects adorned with painted decoration (Fig. 13).

These Syrian and Egyptian objects were not the first gilded and enameled glasses. Hellenistic and Roman glassworkers occasionally used a combination of gold foil and enamel to

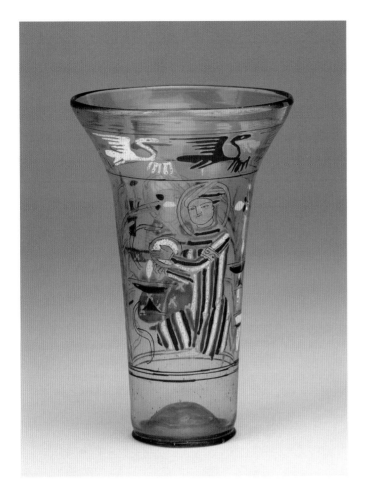

Figure 13
Gilded and enameled beaker decorated with three musicians. Probably made in Syria, about 1250–1275. H. 15.8 cm. Until 1800, the beaker was in the collection of the landgraves of Hessen-Kassel. Hessisches Landesmuseum, Kassel (LÖ 90 A 57).

decorate the surface of glass objects (*Glass of the Caesars* 1987, pp. 261 and 273–275, nos. 150 and 151). Medieval Syrian and Egyptian decorators, on the other hand, made gilded and enameled ornament of extraordinary complexity and in unprecedented numbers. Unlike the Roman objects, Islamic gilded glasses were decorated with powdered gold in an oily medium, which was applied to the surface of the vessel with a brush or a pen. The quality of the painting varies from the painstaking creation of intricate vegetal ornament to bold inscriptions in the calligraphic script known as thuluth.

Almost every kind of Islamic glass vessel may have been gilded and enameled: plates, beakers, bottles, and lamps. Hanging lamps, commissioned by wealthy and influential patrons to illuminate the interiors of mosques, mausoleums, and madrasas (Qur'anic schools), survive in large numbers. Some of these objects bear the names of donors who appear in the historical record. Many mosque lamps, therefore, are datable, and they provide us with a key to understanding the development of styles of decoration through more than two centuries.

The evidence of datable lamps and other objects shows that the earliest Islamic gilded and enameled glasses were made in Syria in the 12th century. Carl Johan Lamm (1929–30) constructed an elaborate and largely hypothetical typology of Islamic enameled glass, which he attributed to workshops in the Syrian cities of Raqqa, Aleppo, and Damascus. Today, few scholars subscribe to Lamm's classification, and there is little agreement about exactly where particular objects were made (*Glass of the Sultans* 2001, pp. 199–207). It is clear, however, that they were produced in Syria.

As far as we know, no mosque lamps were imported into western Europe—there would have been no use for them—but beakers and bottles reached many parts of Europe as objects of prestige or veneration: a 13th-century flask in the Dom- und Diözesanmuseum, Vienna, Austria, for example, has been revered since 1365 because it was believed to contain earth stained with the blood of the Holy Innocents (*ibid*., pp. 249–252, no. 124). From time to time, archeological excavations in Europe bring to light fragments of Islamic gilded and enameled glass, often from contexts attributed for other reasons to aristocratic or merchant families. Wenzel (1984), for example, described fragments of a beaker decorated with an Arabic inscription, a Muslim blazon (coat of arms), and a frieze of horsemen. A smaller number of objects, mostly beakers, have survived above ground and in the cabinets of the rich; they include a beaker, also with horsemen (**114**), reputedly discovered in the altar of a medieval church at Orvieto, in central Italy.

HEDWIG BEAKERS

112 belongs to a small but famous group of vessels. They share several characteristics: the same form (they are beakers with a straight, tapering side), the same finishing techniques (they were decorated by cutting), and the same shallow faceting of the upper wall in order to display the ornament in relief (Figs. 14 and 15). The beakers range in height from 8.3 to 14.6 centimeters. All are colorless or nearly colorless. The repertoire of motifs is varied: lions, eagles, griffins, and the tree of life are recurrent elements, but we also find a chalice, a crescent moon and stars, palmettes, and abstract or geometric motifs.

According to separate traditions, two of these beakers are associated with the wife of Duke Henry I of Silesia and Poland, Saint Hedwig (1174–1243), who was canonized in 1267—hence the collective names for such objects: *Hedwigsgläser* (Hedwig glasses) and, more recently, *Hedwigsbecher* (Hedwig beakers).

The legend of Saint Hedwig is described in a manuscript written at the court of Duke Ludwig I of Liegnitz and Brieg in 1353. According to the legend, Duke Henry criticized his pious wife for her ascetic habits and in particular for drinking water instead of wine (Fig. 16). Determined to make her change her ways, he unexpectedly confronted her while she was dining and snatched the cup from her hand. When he drank from the cup, he realized that the water it contained had been transformed into wine. One tradition associates this miracle with the Hedwig beaker in the cathedral at Cracow, Poland, while another associates it with a beaker formerly in the National Museum in Wrocław, Poland, which disappeared in 1944.

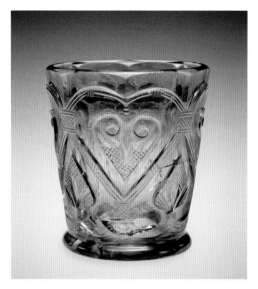

Figure 14
Hedwig beaker, blown, wheel-cut. Place of manufacture uncertain, perhaps Sicily, late 12th century. H. 14.1 cm The British Museum, London
(1959.4-14.1).

Figure 15
Asseburg Hedwig beaker, blown, cut, polished,
engraved. Place of manufacture uncertain, perhaps Sicily, late 12th century. H. 10.2 cm. Private
collection, Germany.

Figure 16
Saint Hedwig drinking water instead of wine. From a manuscript of 1353. The J. Paul
Getty Museum, Los Angeles (Ms. Ludwig XI 7 f.30v, acc. no. 83.MN.126.30v).

Thirteen Hedwig beakers are, or once were, in church treasuries in Europe. Fragments of up to 11 others have been found in archeological excavations, all in Europe. Two of the beakers that have survived above ground, in the treasury of the monastery of Saint Nicolas d'Oignies, preserved in the convent of the Soeurs de Notre Dame in Namur, Belgium, are said to have arrived as gifts of Jacques de Vitry, bishop of Acre from 1216 to 1226 (although the list of the bishop's gifts does not specify any glass). They have mounts made in and after 1228. One of the excavated fragments, from Novogrudok, Belarus, is reported to have come from a 12th-century context; another fragment, from Hilpoltstein, Germany, was found in a context attributed to the years 1170–1180, while a third, from Pistoia, Italy, is from a deposit datable to the decades around 1300. Thus the known find-places of Hedwig beakers are in Europe, and the earliest datable examples belong to the 12th or early 13th century.

From the moment the Hedwig beakers attracted scholarly attention, the place of their manufacture has been the subject of considerable debate. The following paragraphs contain a list of suggested places of manufacture, together with brief comments. The list is long: (1) the Islamic world, (2) Novogrudok, (3) Byzantium, (4) central Europe, (5) southern Italy, (6) the Latin East, and (7) Sicily.

1. *The Islamic world.* Several scholars have compared the ornament on Hedwig glasses with that of rock crystal objects made in Egypt during the reign of the Fatimids (969–1171) and concluded that the beakers were made in the Islamic world: in Egypt, Syria, or Iran. However, no fragment of a Hedwig glass has been reported from Egypt or Western Asia, despite the recovery of many hundreds, if not thousands, of relief-cut glass fragments from Fusṭāṭ, Nishapur, and other places. In any case, Hedwig glasses, which have thick walls and are boldly cut, are unlike almost all Islamic glass and rock crystal objects, which have paper-thin walls and fine lines.

2. *Novogrudok.* The discovery of a fragmentary Hedwig glass and, "nearby," a small piece of unworked glass of the same color led Shelkovnikov (1966, pp. 109–112) to reject the view that the glasses are Islamic and to attribute them to a local workshop. Nevertheless, we may discount the possibility that the Hedwig glasses were made at Novogrudok on the grounds that the find-place is some 400 miles/640 kilometers from the next specimen (in the cathedral at Cracow) and it is difficult to imagine the circumstances in which objects made in Belarus reached sites in Germany and Italy.

3. *Byzantium.* The notion that Hedwig beakers are Byzantine derives from three hypotheses. The first of these is that the beakers were among luxury items produced at Constantinople and from time to time sent as gifts to rulers in the West. The second hypothesis maintains that they were brought to western Europe as part of the dowry of Theophanu, daughter of the Byzantine Emperor John I Tzimisces, when she married the Holy Roman Emperor Otto II in 972. Finally, Philippe (1970, pp. 125–141) and others noted that booty from the sack of Constantinople in 1204, preserved in the Treasury of San Marco in Venice, includes a number of relief-cut glasses. However, only one of these objects (a bowl decorated with lions: *Glass of the Sultans* 2001, pp. 178–179, no. 84) even remotely resembles a Hedwig glass, and, in any

case, scholars are still undecided about the date and origin of many of the San Marco glasses. The evidence in favor of the view that Hedwig beakers are Byzantine, therefore, is purely circumstantial.

4. *Central Europe.* More recently, some scholars have maintained that the Hedwig beakers were made in central Europe and are medieval or, in most cases, modern. We may safely reject the explanation that they are modern. Seven of the glasses have 13th- to 15th-century metal mounts, and archeological excavations have yielded additional examples from medieval contexts.

Similarly, despite the exclusively European distribution of the Hedwig glasses, the explanation that they were made in central or eastern Europe in the Middle Ages is untenable. Chemical analyses of six examples show that they are made of soda-lime glass, and this alone would render them very unusual if they had been made in Europe in the later medieval period, when glassmakers habitually produced potash glasses (see pages 66–68).

5. *Southern Italy.* The late Basil Gray believed that the technique used to finish the Hedwig beakers was derived from Islamic glass cutters. At the same time, he was puzzled by the wholly un-Islamic distribution of the surviving examples. Consequently, Gray sought an origin in one of the melting pots of Mediterranean cultures: southern Italy. Hedwig glasses, he maintained (in a colloquium at Basel in 1988), were made in the reign of the Hohenstaufen emperor Frederick II (1194–1250), either in Sicily or on the mainland of southern Italy. Later, Pinder-Wilson (1991, p. 128) likened the lions, eagles, and griffins on some Hedwig beakers to the same creatures "seen on the exteriors and interiors of the churches of south Italy."

6. *The Latin East.* Saldern (1996, pp. 239–242) suggested that the beakers were made in the Latin East at the time of the Crusades and were taken to Europe by crusaders, pilgrims, or merchants. He noted that tradition associates the two Hedwig beakers at Namur with Jacques de Vitry, bishop of Acre between 1216 and 1226 (but see above), and that a fragment excavated on the site of the royal palace in Budapest *may* have been brought home by King Andrew II, who collected relics in the Holy Land in 1217. In this context, it is noteworthy that Wedepohl (2005) and Wedepohl and others (2007), on the basis of chemical analyses of six Hedwig beakers and their similarity to analyses of certain Islamic low-magnesium soda-ash glasses, concluded that the objects were made in the Levant. We know, however, that raw glass was exported from the Levant between the 11th and 13th centuries, and so the conclusion that the raw glass was made in the Levant is not necessarily at odds with the view that the beakers were produced elsewhere (see below).

7. *Sicily.* Despite the similarities that unite the Hedwig glasses, their ornament falls into two distinct groups: (A) beakers decorated with, among other things, one or two lions, plus an eagle and/or a griffin, or a "tree of life" motif; and (B) beakers decorated with palmettes, crescents, or geometric motifs, but neither animals nor birds. All four of the main motifs in Group A have Christological significance. Hedwig glasses, therefore, are not only un-Islamic in form and execution, but at least some of them are also non-Islamic in purpose. Indeed, so

appropriate are the form and (in Group A) the decoration for incorporation in monstrances and chalices that it is logical to infer that this was their primary function; indeed, in Groups A and B, seven Hedwig glasses are known to have served these purposes by the 15th century, and the feet of six others are notched for attachment to metal mounts. Thus, we may reasonably suspect that the owners of Hedwig glasses were Christian.

Recently, a number of rock crystal objects have been associated with the *nobiles officinae* (noble workshops) at the court of the Norman kings at Palermo, Sicily. Distelberger (2004, pp. 109–113) attributed rock crystal vessels to the Palermo workshops and noted that the facets on some of them are similar to the facets on the Hedwig beakers. Indeed, the Hedwig beakers, he concluded, are Sicilian (Distelberger 2005; see also Kröger 2006). If this is so, they were made with raw glass imported from the Levant (William of Tyre, writing before 1185, noted that "the glass [of Tyre] is exported to distant provinces, and it provides material suitable for vessels that are remarkable and of outstanding clarity": Carboni, Lacerenza, and Whitehouse 2003, p. 146).

While there are parallels in Apulia for images on Hedwig beakers, equally close or closer parallels are found in the decoration of buildings constructed by the Norman kings of Sicily (Tronzo 1997). The ceiling mosaic of the Stanza Normanna in the Norman palace at Palermo, for example, includes lions, griffins, and an eagle that resemble the creatures on some of the Hedwig beakers. The mosaic, and perhaps the beakers, were made in the reign of William II (1166–1189).

Thus it is attractive to attribute the Hedwig beakers to Sicily, perhaps during the reign of William II. If this is correct, can we explain the presence of most of these Sicilian objects in central Europe? The answer is, yes. In 1177, William II arranged the marriage of his aunt, Constance, to Henry VI, son of the Holy Roman Emperor Frederick Barbarossa, whose family, the Hohenstaufen, were extraordinarily powerful in central Europe. Henry became king of Sicily in 1194. The "migration" of Palermitan luxury goods to central Europe in the late 12th century, therefore, is explicable in terms of Constance's dowry when she married Henry, or of the subsequent movement of treasures between the many branches of the Hohenstaufen family. The earliest archeological find of a Hedwig beaker, from Hilpoltstein, discovered in a context attributed to the years 1170–1180, is consistent with this hypothesis.

VESSELS USED IN SACRED SPACES

Fragments of Hedwig beakers have been found in secular contexts (Lierke 2005, pp. 103–106, provides a list of finds from archeological excavations, mostly at royal or aristocratic residences), but several beakers have survived above ground because they were used as chalices or monstrances. Hedwig beakers therefore provide a stepping stone from the objects for domestic use, described on pages 33–48, to objects for use in sacred spaces. The following pages contain notes on lamps, chalices, reliquaries, and glass vessels placed in Christian graves.

Lamps

We have abundant pictorial evidence for the use of glass lamps (Fig. 17) to illuminate churches and synagogues, and presumably similar lamps were also used in domestic contexts.

Late medieval paintings, especially in northern and central Italy, depict two types of lamps. The first of these has a more or less globular body and a series of small vertical handles around the midpoint that were intended to receive the hooks of a metal lamp hanger (Fig. 18). Such lamps were suspended singly from ceilings or horizontal beams. The second type has a shallow bowl and a narrow stem that was inserted into a polycandelon (a suspended metal frame containing several identical lamps) (Fig. 19).

The first type of lamp is found mainly in southern Europe, from the Balkans to Spain, with rare outliers farther north. One of these outliers is a fragmentary lamp from Knaresborough Castle in North Yorkshire, U.K. (Tyson 2000, pp. 147–148, no. g476). Such lamps are sometimes described as being of Islamic type because the form resembles that of an Islamic mosque lamp, the best-known examples of which were made between the 13th and 15th centuries, and they have elaborate gilded and enameled ornament (*Glass of the Sultans* 2001, pp. 226–238, nos. 113–118). Indeed, the lamp from Knaresborough has been described more than once as an import from the Islamic world. The form, however, is found in the Mediterranean region in Moslem, Jewish, and Christian contexts (cf. *A travers le verre* 1989, p. 352, no. 397; and Lusuardi Siena and Zuech 2000), and its origin is not yet certain; perhaps it is a

Figure 17
Hanging lamps in the Tomb of the Virgin Mary, Jerusalem.

Figure 18
Hanging lamps. From the
Sister Haggadah (about 1350).
The British Library, London
(Or 2884 f.17v).

Figure 19
Hanging lamps. From a
fresco by Giotto di Bondone
(1303–1305). Scrovegni
Chapel, Padua.

distant descendant of the suspended bowl lamps of the late Roman period (e.g., *Glass of the Caesars* 1987, pp. 204–205, no. 113). Among the earliest representations of this type of lamp are three examples above the altar of the Palatine Chapel, Palermo, in a miniature in the late 12th-century manuscript "Liber ad honorem Augusti" of Peter of Eboli.

The type of lamp that was used in a polycandelon has clear Late Antique antecedents (cf. a brass polycandelon in the Musée du Louvre attributed to the fifth or sixth century: *Byzance* 1992, p. 121, no. 68). In the Middle Ages, it had a much wider distribution than hanging lamps in western Europe, extending from the Mediterranean to northern Germany and the British Isles. At the same time, outside Europe, it was commonly used in the Islamic world, from Egypt (Scanlon and Pinder-Wilson 2001, pp. 53–55, no. 25a and b) to Iran. Stiaffini (1999, p. 119), noting that such lamps are very often found during excavations at medieval churches and monasteries, suggested that they may have been used almost exclusively in religious buildings. Similarly, more than half of the glass lamps found in England have been recovered from the sites of monasteries (Tyson 2000, p. 143). Nevertheless, their presence in secular contexts is also well attested in Germany (e.g., *Phönix aus Sand und Asche* 1988, p. 437, no. 551, from Lübeck), France (e.g., *A travers le verre* 1989, p. 346, no. 388), and the British Isles (e.g., many of the examples published by Tyson 2000, pp. 145–147, nos. g363–g475).

Chalices

By the 15th century, four Hedwig beakers are known to have been attached to metal mounts. The support made the beaker available for use as a chalice or as a monstrance (a vessel for displaying the Host or relics) (see pages 51–52). This is remarkable, given that, from the pontificate of Leo IV (r. 847–855), priests were instructed that "nullus in ligneo, plumbeo, et vitro calice audeat missam celebrare" (let no one dare to celebrate the Mass with a wood, lead, or glass chalice) (quoted by Kraus and Sauer 1897, p. 486, n. 3). Perhaps this prohibition was ignored in northern Europe. Or is it possible that these rare glasses, probably from the royal workshops of Palermo, which also produced hard stone vessels, were mistakenly believed to be rock crystal?

Reliquaries

From the early days of the Church, saints and their relics (that is, parts of their bodies or objects associated with them) were revered. Saints were believed to perform miracles with divine assistance and so people sought their aid to undo the consequences of sin, to cure illness, and to cause things to turn out for the best. They were honored by feasts on the anniversaries of their deaths. The shrines of saints and their relics (literally, "things left behind") often became destinations for pilgrims. Items brought into contact with relics (such as oil from lamps burning above a saint's shrine) were also venerated, and pilgrims would take them home as evidence of their devotion.

The veneration of saints' relics took many forms, from pilgrimage to famous shrines, such as that of Saint James at Santiago de Compostela, Spain, to worship at altars that contained fragmentary relics of local saints, placed there when the altars were consecrated.

The cult of relics enjoyed great popularity in the two centuries after 1000. Many ancient monasteries were reformed in this period, and, in the process, the cults of their traditional patron saints were renewed. The number of pilgrims increased. In the 1130s, Abbot Suger of Saint-Denis, near Paris, recorded that he had to rebuild his abbey because pilgrims filled the church to the point of overflowing.

In late Roman times, the majority of saints were men. In the 10th and 11th centuries, cults of female saints became prominent in western Christendom. Abbot Geoffrey (d. 1052) rediscovered the relics of Mary Magdalene at Vézeley, France, no later than 1050, and in 1155 graves found outside the walls of Cologne, Germany, were identified as those of Saint Ursula and her 11,000 virgin martyrs, a discovery that quickly provided relics for churches all over Europe.

In the later Middle Ages, it became customary to recognize recently deceased figures as saints. Saint Hedwig of Silesia, for example, was canonized in 1267, only 24 years after her death (see page 48). The cult of saints had grown and diversified, and it attracted pilgrims from all walks of life. *The Canterbury Tales* by Geoffrey Chaucer (about 1342–1400) describes a group of pilgrims traveling from London to Canterbury to visit the shrine of Saint Thomas à Becket. They include both rich and poor, and both ignorant and educated.

Depending on the amount of veneration accorded to a relic and the wealth of the donor who provided the container to preserve and display it, a reliquary might be a gilded and gem-encrusted casket or a simple beaker of forest glass sealed with beeswax. Three Hedwig beakers—two from the treasury of the Soeurs de Notre Dame at Namur, Belgium, and one in the cathedral at Halberstadt, Germany—have metal mounts with covers, and they were used as monstrances. The beaker at Halberstadt, for example, contained relics of the apostles James and Thomas (Lamm 1929–30, p. 174, no. 7).

Glass Vessels in Christian Graves

Glass vessels are found in one other, unexpected late medieval religious context: Christian cemeteries. The custom of placing glasses in graves was by no means common; indeed, it was confined to a few small regions, such as parts of southwestern France and northeastern Spain (Foy and Démians d'Archimbaud 1996).

The range of forms is small: bottles and flasks, goblets, and a few open vessels. The bottles and flasks may have contained holy water. The open forms seem to have been lamps; examples were found in the graves of several church dignitaries buried in the cathedral at Angers, France. The goblets are assumed to have been buried with priests as substitutes for chalices used during Mass, since the Church forbade the use of glass chalices (see page 55). One goblet, from Saint-Genest at Nevers, France, was accompanied by a glass plate that served as a substitute for a paten.

VESSELS USED FOR SCIENTIFIC AND MEDICAL PURPOSES

In the 12th and 13th centuries, Latin translations of treatises by ancient Greek and Muslim scientists began to circulate in Europe, providing a huge impetus for local scholars. Two fields in which this new knowledge benefited directly from developments in glassmaking were experimental science and medicine. Experimental science came to depend on glass apparatus that was transparent and did not contaminate its contents by corroding. In medicine, which employed similar apparatus in the preparation of substances for treating disease, transparent flasks were essential for uroscopy (see pages 59–60). Another result of the increasing use of glass for experimental purposes was the emergence of optics as a branch of science and the development of mirrors (Fig. 20) and lenses, which led directly to the invention of a tool that even today is indispensable: spectacles (Macfarlane and Martin 2002, pp. 38–43).

Figure 20
Windowpanes and convex mirror. Detail from Jan van Eyck, *The Arnolfini Wedding* (dated 1434). The National Gallery, London.

Distillers' Apparatus

Distillation is a method of separating a mixture of two or more substances into its components. When the dissolved substances are heated, the most volatile component (the one with the lowest boiling point) vaporizes first. This vapor cools and condenses, creating a distillate for collection. The residue of the original mixture contains the less volatile components. The practice of distillation was introduced to Europe from the Islamic world: hence the adoption of the Arabic word for a still (see below).

Although distillation seems to have been practiced in Italy from about 1100, few examples of medieval distilling apparatus have survived. Medieval stills had two principal uses: for preparing acids and other substances used in alchemy, and for distilling alcohol. In his "Tractatus de vinis" (Treatise on wines), Arnaldo of Villanova, who died about 1313, describes the distillation of wine mixed with herbs and spices to make liqueurs such as rosolio, which was flavored with raisins and sundew.

We know from medieval and early modern treatises that, apart from a source of heat, most medieval stills consisted of three elements (Fig. 21). The liquid mixture awaiting distillation was placed in a flask, often known as a cucurbit (from Latin *cucurbita*, "gourd") on account of its shape, above the heat source. On top of the cucurbit was a vessel designed to trap the

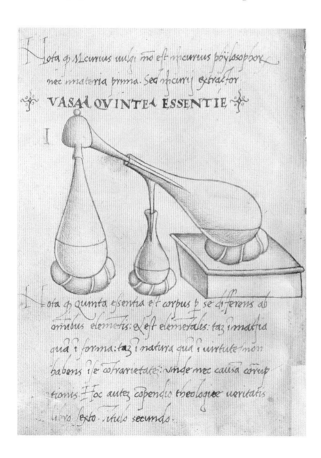

Figure 21
Distilling apparatus. From the Italian manuscript "Miscellanea di alchimia" (16th century). Padua University Library (Ms. 63, f.16v).

vapor that rose from the boiling liquid and to cause it to condense. This was the alembic (from Arabic *al-anbiq,* "still"). The alembic had a neck at the bottom, a rounded top, and a narrow spout that pointed downward. The neck was placed over the mouth of the cucurbit, and the gap between the two was carefully sealed. The vapor was trapped in the alembic, where it condensed and the condensate escaped through the spout. The third element, placed below the end of the spout, was a vessel known as the receiver because it received the distillate. Figure 21 shows a still with two receivers.

The most readily recognizable part of the still is the alembic, and because of its distinctive shape, even small fragments of the neck and shoulder may be identified with confidence. Perhaps the earliest datable example of a European glass alembic consists of fragments from a late 14th-century context in the Palazzo Vitelleschi at Tarquinia, in central Italy (Whitehouse 1987, p. 327, no. 27; Newby 2000, p. 262, no. 7d). Mid-15th-century alembics and cucurbits were excavated at Selborne Priory, Hampshire, U.K. (Moorhouse 1972, pp. 98–101). A 15th- or 16th-century cucurbit is in the Hessisches Landesmuseum Darmstadt in Germany (*Phönix aus Sand und Asche* 1988, p. 435, no. 549), and 16th-century alembics have been found in Strasbourg, France, and Lübeck, Germany (*ibid.,* pp. 434–435, nos. 547 and 548).

Flasks for Uroscopy

Uroscopy (the visual examination of urine) was a widespread method of medical diagnosis. Doctors relied upon the color and clarity of their patients' urine to identify diseases and suggest treatments. Samples were collected in glass flasks that, ideally, were colorless and of even thickness to permit accurate observation. Knowledge of uroscopy in medieval Europe was probably acquired, together with other medical practices, from the Islamic world through such institutions as the famous Schola Medica Salernitana (Salerno Medical School), which already existed at Salerno, in southern Italy, in the ninth century. This knowledge was disseminated throughout Europe by way of monasteries, itinerant physicians, and medical schools attached to newly founded universities such as Paris (established in 1150), Bologna (1158), Oxford (1167), Montpellier (1181), and Padua (1222).

The color of urine was considered to be one of the most important means of diagnosing illness, and Newby (1999, p. 119) quotes from a 14th-century guide to uroscopy: "Reds, ranging from crocus-color to that of intense fire, signify excesses of the digestion. Colors resembling those of liver, white leaves or cabbage stalks indicate overheating. Black and leaden colors indicate bad digestion. The colors of spring water, light filtered through horn, milk, or camel hair show indigestion. Pallid colors like cooked fat indicate the beginnings of digestion. Cider colors show medium digestion. Golden colors alone are the sign of a perfect digestion."

Miniature paintings in medieval manuscripts, beginning with the image of the Norman king William II on his deathbed in 1189, depict physicians practicing uroscopy. The physician holds the glass flask containing the sample at arm's length, observing it against the light (Fig.

Figure 22
Miniature depicting William II, the Norman king of Sicily, on his deathbed in 1189.
At the left is a doctor inspecting a urine sample. From Peter of Eboli, "Liber ad
honorem Augusti" (1196). Burgerbibliothek, Bern (Cod. 120, f.97).

22). Thanks to these illustrations, archeologists have identified pouch- and pear-shaped flasks,
found in excavations, as intended for uroscopy.

Lenses and Spectacles

In 1268, Roger Bacon (about 1220–1292), an English friar who knew the work of Alhazen,
an Arab polymath and student of optics, recorded the following observation in his "Opus
majus": "If the letters of a book or any minute objects be viewed through a lesser segment of
a sphere of glass or crystal, whose plane base is laid upon them, they will appear far better
and larger. . . . And therefore this instrument is useful to old men and to those that have weak
eyes" (quoted by Macfarlane and Martin 2002, p. 37). The "lesser segment of a sphere of glass"
with a "plane base," of course, is a plano-convex lens.

Reading glasses, consisting of pairs of lenses assembled for wearing in front of the eyes,
were invented within a generation of Bacon's observation. In 1289, writing in Florence, Italy,
Sandro di Popozo noted, in his "Traité de la conduit de la famille" (Treatise on leading [i.e.,
being head of] the family), "I am so debilitated by age that without the glasses known as
spectacles, I would no longer be able to read and write." Sandro's spectacles were a recent

invention. The Dominican friar Giordano da Rivalto (1260–1311), preaching a sermon in Pisa in 1306, stated, "It is not yet 20 years since the art of making spectacles, one of the most useful arts on earth, was discovered." Taken together, the two statements suggest that the first pairs of spectacles were made somewhere in central Italy in the 1280s.

Although (as far as I am aware) no very early spectacles have survived above ground or come to light in archeological excavations, we know what they looked like. In 1352, Tommaso da Modena painted a series of portraits in the chapter house of the convent of San Nicolò at Treviso, in northern Italy. Two of his subjects have single lenses to improve their sight; one is on a long handle, and the other is mounted on a stand. A third subject, Cardinal Hugh of Provence, is depicted wearing spectacles (Fig. 23). The lenses are mounted in circular frames with short handles (they resemble modern magnifying glasses). The ends of the handles are perforated and tied or riveted together. The frames, therefore, are connected by a hinged attachment that sits on the bridge of the wearer's nose. (Figure 24 shows a mohel wearing similar spectacles.) This was a brilliant invention, and for more than 700 years, the lives of countless millions of people have been transformed by spectacles.

Figure 23
Cardinal wearing spectacles. Detail from fresco by Tommaso da Modena (1352). Chapter house of the convent of San Nicolò, Treviso.

Figure 24
Mohel (a person who circumcises male infants according to Jewish ritual) wearing spectacles. Detail from the Master of the Tucher Altar, *The Circumcision of Christ* (1450). Suermondt-Ludwig-Museum, Aachen.

Glassmaking in Europe between A.D. 500 and 1500

Karl Hans Wedepohl

DURING THE POST-ROMAN PERIOD, glasshouses in Europe continued to produce soda-lime glass according to the Roman recipe until about A.D. 800 to 900. Roman glassmaking was characterized by a strict adherence to the same proportions of quartz sand (mainly from rivers), natron (trona, $Na_3CO_3HCO_3 \cdot 2H_2O$) from the Egyptian Wadi el Natrun, and lime (mainly from seashells) for the batches of glass melts. Pliny the Elder had suggested the use of river sand for quartz and shells for lime. Studies of Roman glass from the imperial period have not revealed substantial changes in chemical composition at different times or in different regions. The average composition of 781 Roman glasses from Europe and the Near East is given in Table 1. Because of the absence of sizable deviations from this average composition, several authors, including Nenna, Picon, and Vichy (2000) and Freestone (2003), have assumed that Roman and comparable raw glass was made in a small number of glasshouses. Recent investigations of Roman glass in Europe have provided more details on the origin of the raw glass (mostly in the Levant and Egypt). Large sets of analytical data on historical glass relevant to the subject of this chapter have been published by Brill (1999) and Wedepohl (2003).

Soda-lime glass continued to be employed for making window glass for monasteries and churches in Italy, Germany, England, Norway, and elsewhere during the first millennium A.D. Green and blue were the favored colors (Dell'Acqua 1997), and tesserae with those colors were added to the batch. The Roman origin of these tesserae is demonstrated by their concentrations of antimony oxide, which range from 0.3% to 2.5%. Investigations of glass from Fulda and the Carolingian monastery of Lorsch, both in Germany, and from Zalavár in Hungary showed that this glass contains 8% calcium oxide (CaO) and 16% sodium oxide (Na_2O) instead of the 6.8% calcium oxide and 17.5% sodium oxide in Roman glass. The probable reason for the replacement of a lower amount of sodium oxide with a higher amount of calcium oxide in the Carolingian soda-lime glass was that the availability of natron from Egypt was limited and, at the same time, there was ready access to lime. These levels of lower sodium and higher calcium, as shown in Table 1, can be used for dating.

Islamic glass weights studied by Gratuze and Barrandon (1990) indicate a general change from soda-lime glass to soda-ash glass in Egypt and presumably in other Islamic countries

Glassblowers and furnace. Detail from a manuscript of Pedanius Dioscorides, "Tractatus de herbis" (1458). Biblioteca Estense, Modena (Ms. Lat. 993 = a.L.9.28, f.238r).

Table 1

Average Chemical Composition of Roman and Medieval Glasses

	A	B	C
Object	Roman Soda-Lime Glass	Early Medieval Soda-Lime Glass	Early Wood-Ash Glass
Time	A.D. 0–500	500–900	780–1000
Origin	Germany, England, France, Italy, Greece, Serbia, Israel, Tunisia	Germany, England, Italy, Norway, Hungary	Paderborn, Drudewenshusen, Lorsch, Staré Město-Sady
Number	781	157	6
SiO_2 %	69.4	68.2	57.6
TiO_2	0.12	0.14	0.15
Al_2O_3	2.35	2.47	2.01
Fe_2O_3	0.69	1.0	0.62
MnO	0.56	0.61	1.35
MgO	0.54	0.84	3.71
CaO	6.8	7.5	17.9
Na_2O	17.5	16.5	1.63
K_2O	0.61	0.89	11.8
P_2O_5	0.09	0.14	2.34

D	E	F	G
Wood-Ash Glass	Wood-Ash/Lime Glass	Mixed-Alkali Glass	Late Medieval Soda-Ash Glass
1000–1400	1400–1600	1400–1500	1250–1350
Lorsch, Brunshausen, Höxter, Corvey	Höxter	Taunus	Italy, etc.
17	7	9	57
48.9	51.3	57.1	69.1
0.13	0.20	0.33	0.09
1.64	2.36	1.83	1.40
0.54	0.80	0.96	0.47
1.24	1.10	1.19	0.78
4.07	4.28	3.37	3.39
19.7	25.1	25.7	10.7
0.34	2.20	2.50	11.2
19.4	7.44	2.93	2.15
2.19	4.58	3.21	0.23

of the Near East between the ninth and 10th centuries. This change has been observed in glass objects excavated at Fusṭāṭ (Old Cairo), Egypt. The principal sodium-containing raw material for soda-lime glass was natron from the Wadi el Natrun in Egypt. Any interruption in the exportation of natron from Egypt would have seriously affected the production of glass in Europe. One such interruption occurred in the late first millennium A.D., and European glasshouses replaced the combination of natron and lime with wood ash. Consequently, the new recipe combined potassium and calcium instead of soda and calcium. The large proportion of potassium and calcium in the new glass necessitated an increase in the melting temperature from slightly above 1000°C (for soda-lime glass) to about 1300°C. Wood ash was produced by the burning of beeches, the most common tree in central Europe at that time. A green wood-ash glass fragment was discovered in the imperial palace of Charlemagne at Paderborn, Germany, which was destroyed in a Saxon attack about A.D. 780 (Wedepohl, Winkelmann, and Hartmann 1997).

Potassium-rich glass is softer and weathers more easily than soda glass. It is usually colored green because of ferrous iron in the reducing atmosphere of the furnace. This interferes with the production of other colors in a manner that is not replicated in light soda glass.

Wood-Ash Glass

Studies of the composition of medieval wood-ash glass have shown a systematic increase in the ratios of calcium oxide to potassium oxide (K_2O) over time. The trunks of trees contain more potassium and less calcium than the bark. Twigs have more bark than trunks and are therefore richer in calcium. The lowest ratios of calcium oxide to potassium oxide indicate that large numbers of beech trunks were used for ashing. To save the valuable trunks, more and more twigs were used for ashing in the later Middle Ages. A higher amount of potassium in the ash reflects a lower melting temperature for the batch. A recipe for making wood-ash glass with a low melting temperature, described by the monk Theophilus in his "De diversis artibus" (also known as "Diversarum artium schedula") at the beginning of the 12th century (Theophilus 1961, pp. 39–40), calls for the melting of two parts of ash from beech trunks and one part of quartz sand. Table 1 lists the average composition of 17 wood-ash glasses from excavations at Lorsch, Brunshausen, Höxter, Corvey, and the Steimcke glasshouse in the Bramwald Mountains, all in Germany (Wedepohl 2003). These glasses, produced between A.D. 1000 and 1400, have a low ratio of calcium oxide to potassium oxide, and they were melted at a temperature of about 1200°C. This was the favored method of production during a time when few technological changes appear to have been made. These optimum conditions for making wood-ash glass with a relatively low melting temperature declined as more and more wood was used by a growing population between A.D. 1200 and 1300.

In the 14th and 15th centuries, authorities closely controlled the consumption of wood by glasshouses that were situated near highly populated areas. In the forests of the Spessart

Mountains in Germany, the numbers of glass vessels and windowpanes each glasshouse could make during a given period were strictly regulated. Such regulations resulted in the use of more twigs in glassmaking. This can be observed, for example, in glass produced at the Laudengrund glasshouse in the Spessart Mountains, where the ratio of calcium oxide to potassium oxide increased from 1 to 2 about A.D. 1300. Production at Laudengrund included both wood-ash glass and wood-ash/lime glass, employing both logs and twigs. In later wood-ash/lime glass, the concentration of potassium oxide decreased to 7.5% and the ratio of calcium oxide to potassium oxide increased to 3. In this glass, the low level of potassium had to be supplemented by sodium, applied as sodium chloride, in order to melt the batch. The change in the chemical composition from wood-ash to wood-ash/lime glass caused the melting temperature to increase from 1200°C to 1350°C. The calcium-rich wood-ash/lime glass is harder and more resistant to weathering than the earlier wood-ash glass. Table 1 presents the average composition of seven wood-ash/lime glasses from Höxter, which were made between the 15th and 17th centuries and later.

The making of the final type of medieval glass involved the use of twigs and branches of beech trees, as well as some lime, resulting in high calcium and low potassium concentrations. The ratios of calcium oxide to potassium oxide in this mixed-alkali glass are close to 9. The low amount of potassium (about 3% potassium oxide) is supplemented by about 2.5% sodium chloride. Experiments by Gerth, Wedepohl, and Heide (1998) have shown that the maximum concentration of sodium chloride soluble in wood-ash glass melts is close to 2.3%. The nine mixed-alkali glasses analyzed in Table 1 came from three late medieval (about A.D. 1450) glasshouses in the Taunus Mountains of Germany.

The composition of early wood-ash glass, produced from about A.D. 780 to 1000, is better understood in light of the later types described above. Chemically, the composition of the early glass is not as consistent as that of the later types. Its ratio of calcium oxide to potassium oxide ranged from 1 to 6, with an average of 1.5. The glassmakers of that time were probably not well informed about the relationship between the composition and melting temperature of wood-ash glass. The average composition of six early wood-ash glasses from Paderborn, Drudewenshusen, and Lorsch in Germany, and from Staré Město-Sady in Moravia, Czech Republic, is given in Table 1.

My most recent investigation of medieval wood-ash glass has dealt with four compositions (early wood-ash, wood-ash, wood-ash/lime, and mixed-alkali glasses), which were produced mainly between 800 and 1000, 1000 and 1400, 1400 and 1600, and 1400 and 1500 respectively. Because not every glasshouse was technically proficient enough to adopt all of the changes in the use of different raw materials (derived from different parts of trees), there was some overlapping of glass types during certain periods. But most of the glasses from excavations can be dated on the basis of the chemical compositions (mainly the ratio of calcium oxide to potassium oxide) listed in Table 1.

In general, the batch ingredients for wood-ash glass are (a) quartz, (b) ash from the trunks and branches of beech trees, and (c) oxides for coloring:

(a) The silica contents of examined glasses range from 49% to 57.5%, indicating that there was not much variation in the proportion of quartz in the batch. Local sands from deposits near the glasshouses in the woods were used.

(b) The ash of beech trees containing potassium was employed as a flux, and calcium was used as a stabilizer. When a large proportion of twigs was part of the beech ash, a few percent of sodium chloride had to be added. The potassium and calcium levels in the trunks and bark of beech trees were based on different constituents in the soils.

Glass from English and French glasshouses often contains distinctly higher concentrations of magnesium and phosphorus than wood-ash glass produced in Germany, as is noted in Table 1. The compositional differences can be explained by the use of fern ash as a substitute for wood ash in Italy, France, and England, since forests were fewer in these countries than in Germany. Data on the compositions of fern-ash glasses have been reported by Jackson and Smedley (2004).

(c) Wood-ash glasses used for medieval church windows were colored by the addition of several metals or metal oxides to the melts. The addition of copper-containing colorants to the melts under reducing and oxidizing conditions in the furnace resulted in red glass and green glass respectively. Cobalt oxide (CoO) in the range of 0.01% to 0.2% (Wedepohl 2003, pp. 190–196) produced blue. Manganese was added for purple glass, and iron sulfide was used to make yellowish panes.

Lead Glass

The production of lead glass in antiquity began about the same time as the making of soda glass, as has been reported by Sayre (1964). The early use of sodium carbonate and lead oxide (PbO) as major ingredients in glass can be explained by their low melting temperature when mixed with silica (1000°C or lower). Lead oxide (65%–85% PbO) mixed with powdered silica formed lead glass at temperatures as low as 750°C (Smart and Glasser 1974, p. 378). The melting temperature of mixtures of wood ash and lead oxide is also below 800°C.

Beads, rings, tesserae, vessels, and windowpanes were made from lead glass and lead/wood-ash glass. During the Viking period, "linen smoothers" of glass high in lead were fashioned from materials mined in the lead deposit at Melle in France. They were dated to the eighth to ninth centuries, and they may have been the first lead glass in Europe. Wedepohl, Krueger, and Hartmann (1995) investigated 47 lead glasses and 11 lead/wood-ash glasses from northwestern Europe. Most of these glasses are green or yellow, and they date from the 12th to 14th centuries. The culmination of that lead glass manufacture occurred in the 13th century.

The abundance of lead glass probably coincided with periods of advanced lead (and silver) mining. According to the interpretation of lead isotopes in the abovementioned glasses, most of the lead ores came from the Harz Mountains and the Eifel region of Germany (Wedepohl 2003, pp. 199–201). Two important properties of lead glass in comparison with wood-ash glass are the brilliant green and yellow colors and the lower melting temperature of the former.

Extent of Glass Production and Importation

Medieval glass producers made many more windowpanes than vessels. Large quantities of glass were transported along rivers. The windows of the Gothic cathedral in Cologne contain 25 tons of mostly wood-ash glass, which probably arrived on boats on the Rhine. As the population increased after A.D. 1200, many large communities developed throughout Europe. The windows of churches and the vessels made between A.D. 1250 and 1500 required at least 40,000 tons of glass (Wedepohl 2003, p. 159), and about 13 million tons of wood would have been needed to heat the furnaces and to produce ash as a raw material. The yearly production of a medieval glasshouse is estimated to have been between five and 10 tons (*ibid.*, p. 149). At the end of 20 years, a glasshouse would have consumed all of the trees within a kilometer of its location, and it would have been forced to relocate.

In the last third of the medieval period, an elite part of the population developed an interest in luxury glass vessels. These were manufactured by a few specialized glasshouses. Because most of the wood-ash glasses had a green color, light soda-ash glass was favored for high-quality glasses. The cobalt blue panes in church windows often consist of soda-ash glass, even if the rest of the glazing employed wood-ash glass. The addition of cobalt to a wood-ash glass melt results in a blue-green rather than blue color. Soda ash imported from Islamic countries was first used in Venice in the second half of the 13th century. At that time, Venice and its ships were the gateway to Europe. Soda-ash glass (column G in Table 1) differs from soda-lime glass (columns A and B in that table) mainly in the higher concentrations of magnesium and potassium that are found in the former. Countries bordering the Mediterranean Sea produced and exported soda ash made from such halophytes as salicornia. The use of special shapes, enameling, other decoration first employed in Islamic countries and later in Venice, and trails and prunts affixed to the vessel wall were a few of the ways in which ordinary vessels were transformed into luxury beakers, goblets, bottles, cups, jugs, and bowls.

Glassblowing in the Middle Ages: Tradition and Innovation

William Gudenrath

BY THE EARLIEST YEARS of the medieval period, blowing had displaced all other techniques as the means of manufacturing glass vessels. The diverse glassworking methods of the ancient world—core forming, fusing, slumping, and a variety of casting processes—had been lost by the sixth century. Glassblowing had become widespread in the Roman world during the first decades of the first century (Grose 1977). This development marked the beginning of a long period (it ended in the 19th century with the advent of mechanical processes) in which every glass vessel was started as a gather of molten glass on the end of a worker's blowpipe. Thus all medieval glass vessels were made by blowing.

Subsequent cultures that have practiced glassblowing owe an incalculable debt to the glassworkers of the Roman period. Their industry had been so creatively restless and productive that very little was left to be discovered and invented by the fourth century. The medieval glass industry was built on the firm foundation of Rome.

There are two basic types of blowing: free blowing and mold blowing. Both of them were practiced by medieval glassmakers. In free blowing, inflated glass is given its final shape using only gravity and centripetal force, combined with the simplest of hand tools (7, 12, 13, 15, 17, and 19). The mastery of free blowing requires great skill and experience. It has traditionally been passed down from father to son, sometimes over many generations. Mold blowing has a number of subcategories. Full-size mold blowing is used to give an inflated mass of hot glass its final size, shape, and (often) decoration in one brief blowing procedure (6, 8, and 90). A soft bubble of glass is lowered into a heat-resistant mold made of ceramic, metal, or even water-soaked wood. The glass is then inflated until it fills the void and hardens (Gudenrath 1991, p. 234, figs. 153–156). A glassblowing mold is frequently constructed in two or more parts that are hinged in order to make it easier to remove the vessel from the mold.

Full-size mold blowing, so widely used in workshops of the Roman period, was comparatively little used in the medieval period. Dip molding, often called optic molding (20, 30, 44, 53–58, and 63–71), was commonly practiced at that time. In this decorative process, a gather of glass that had been partly inflated was immediately lowered into a mold made of ceramic or metal, then forcefully inflated further to fill the mold (Gudenrath 2001, pp. 59–60, figs. 30–43). The relief pattern inside the mold, typically vertical ribs or a diamond pattern, was transferred to the glass. Because the glass was left in the mold for only a second or so, it

Forest glass workshop. Detail from illustration
shown on page 43.

was still soft when it came out of the mold, and it was further inflated and shaped to create the final product.

Another, completely different mold process was insertion molding, sometimes called fin molding (**58**, **59**, **68**, and **69**). When it was employed, this was the last action taken by the glassworker before the vessel was broken free of the pontil and placed in the annealing oven. With all of the other shaping completed, the entire liquid-holding part of the vessel was reheated until it was slightly soft. It was then lowered onto the fin mold, which instantly transformed the shape of the object's cross section from round to hexagonal or octagonal (Gudenrath 1991, p. 233, fig. 152).

A number of decorative techniques that were not necessarily invented during the Middle Ages were nevertheless so widely employed as to be generally associated with that period. This is true, for example, of prunts—to such a degree that the prunted beaker is, for many re-enactors and enthusiasts, the iconic glass object of that age (**22–29**, **43**, **46**, **47**, **52**, **72**, **74–85**, **88**, and **94–96**). Prunts are small blobs of glass, applied to the outside of a glass vessel, that are sometimes tooled or embossed with a design. They served both decorative and functional purposes: greasy hands could better grip a prunted beaker during meals that were eaten without the aid of utensils.

The finger cup is a more elaborate kind of prunt. A bit of hot glass was applied to the side of the vessel while it was still attached to the blowpipe. When the newly added glass had resoftened the wall, it was sucked inward to form a small cavity (Gudenrath 1991, p. 241, figs. 210–214). Such bits are often accompanied by milled trails[1] on later German vessels. Here, they would have been particularly useful because many of these vessels are huge and staggeringly heavy. It would have been difficult—even dangerous—to pass such objects without these "grips."

Equally iconic of the medieval period are fifth- and sixth-century Frankish beakers with claw prunts (**14**). Claw beakers are similar to finger cups, but here the applied bit of glass was blown outward to form a bulge that was gripped with tweezers and then pulled out and down to rejoin the vessel at a lower point. Additional inflation made the claw smooth and round. A vertical trail was often added to the claw and then milled (*ibid.*, pp. 240–241, figs. 205–209).

In the early Middle Ages, many glasshouses operated independently over a wide area. Only gradually did regional aesthetic commonalities evolve. Later medieval production—luxury objects made for the elite and utilitarian domestic ware crafted for the masses—has customarily been divided into two broad categories: western production for the Christian world and eastern production for the Muslim world.

---

1. A trail (thread) that is milled has been decorated with closely spaced parallel grooves made with a notched wheel that is sometimes called a roulette.

Both of these glassworking cultures produced important innovations. Islamic workshops invented glass staining in the seventh or eighth century, and during the 13th and 14th centuries, they practiced gilding and enameling with unprecedented elaboration and excellence. In the west, two highly original and clever inventions both facilitated and improved the glassmaking process. The remainder of this chapter discusses these inventions, considers their probable origins, describes how they were employed, and assesses their significance. The information is based largely on the results of experiments carried out by the author at the glass furnace.

The Kick

The kick is a substantial, upward-pointing dent in the bottom of a glass vessel. A great variety of medieval glass beakers feature prominent—sometimes amusingly tall—kicks (**19**). Most other vessel types of that period also have kicks in their bases: bowls and bottles (**30**), and even footed vessels such as *Stangengläser* (**55–59**) and *Scheuern* (**87** and **88**), in which the kicks are not so readily discernible.

The kick was formed about halfway through the glassblowing process: just before the vessel was transferred from the blowpipe to the pontil (Figs. 1–3).[2] In preparing to make the kick, the glassblower flattened the bottom of the vessel. Then the blowpipe was turned as one blade of the jacks—the primary hand tool of the glassblower—was pressed into the center of the base. If the tool was held at an upward angle (in relation to the blowpipe), the kick would be conical (as is shown in Figures 1–3 and, for example, **19** and **23**). Alternatively, if the tool remained in alignment with the blowpipe, the kick would be more pointed and would have distinctly curving sides. The most extreme kicks are of the latter type (**30**).

A quick look through any publication on medieval glass (including this one) will reveal that most of the vessels have kicks (Rademacher 1933; *Phönix aus Sand und Asche* 1988; *A travers le verre* 1989). A similar cursory review of standard reference works on Roman glass tells a very different story: comparatively few vessels have true kicks (Isings 1957; *Glass of the Caesars* 1987; Whitehouse 1997, 2001, and 2003). When the bottom of a Roman glass vessel was not left perfectly flat, it was often made with only a slight concavity. This was probably done to prevent a rough or even sharp pontil mark from marring the surface on which the finished vessel stood. It also allowed the vessel to stand on a surface with more stability. This slight concavity is subtle and easy to miss in Roman glass; in medieval glass, the kick is often the most striking feature of an otherwise unremarkable vessel.

2. For a complete photographic sequence of the process of making a similar medieval beaker, see Gudenrath 1991, pp. 223–225, figs. 65–87.

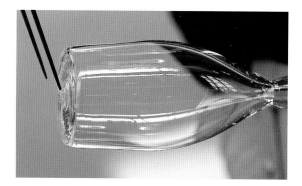

Forming a Conical Kick in the Base of a Vessel

Figure 1
The body of the beaker has been blown and shaped with a constriction near the blowpipe. The base has been flattened and is still soft. While the blowpipe is turned, one blade of the jacks is pressed into the center of the base.

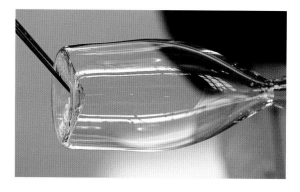

Figure 2
As the turning and pressing continue, the kick becomes taller.

Figure 3
When the required height has been reached, the procedure is stopped. The tumbler is then completed and annealed. (See Figures 6–18 for two possible processes for shaping the vessel's upper half.)

It may not be safe to say that the kick originated as late as the medieval period, but it certainly became part of standard glass workshop practice throughout western Europe during that time.

When a glassblower made a kick in the base of a vessel, he probably did so for a specific purpose, quite apart from helping the vessel to stand securely while preventing the marring of the surface on which it was placed, as was noted above. A kick also makes a vessel marginally stronger and more resistant to breakage if something heavy (such as an ice cube) is casually tossed into it. Certainly, modern bottles whose contents are pressurized (champagne bottles, for example) benefit greatly by not having weaker flat bottoms. (The often-repeated argument that the purpose of a kick in a bottle is to surreptitiously reduce the vessel's volume, providing a savings for an unscrupulous vendor, is, at least in modern times, false: the liquid in the bottle is typically sold by a stated volume, not by the apparent size of the container.)

Could the prominent kicks in medieval glass vessels have been made purely for aesthetic reasons, as a fundamental and unavoidable part of the workers' design vocabulary? This seems unlikely for at least two reasons: (1) household vessels made of other materials, such as ceramic and metal, typically have flat bottoms,[3] and (2) the shape of many medieval glass vessels makes it difficult, if not impossible, to see the kicks. The purpose of the kick seems clearly to have been entirely functional and essential for the success of the manufacturing process.

A continuing experiment that I initiated, somewhat inadvertently, in August 1988 may help to explain why so many medieval glass vessels have kicks. It began while I was practicing at the furnace in preparation for making a video about the manufacturing and decorating processes of the Aldrevandin beaker (see page 41). I made about 20 beaker blanks and left them unannealed on a metal-topped table. While my attention was focused on the more difficult parts of the process, I completely forgot to put kicks in about half of these blanks. At the end of the day, all of the beakers with flat bottoms had shattered because of rapid cooling. This was no surprise: upon the completion of any hot-glassworking process, objects must be cooled slowly and evenly in an annealing oven. After a few hours, the work is removed from the oven, free of stresses that would otherwise likely cause cracks and breakage.

By contrast (I thought it was amazing at the time), all of the beaker blanks with kicks survived intact. It appeared that the kicks had protected the beakers from the ill effects of thermal shock. The next day, I made five Aldrevandin beaker blanks and placed them, unannealed, in a box. Sometime after 2000, one of them broke, but the other four remain intact (Fig. 4). This experiment will run indefinitely.

As a cylindrical or conical vessel cools rapidly, a disparity quickly develops in the contraction that takes place between the wall and the base. Stress is concentrated in the area where they meet, and if that stress exceeds the tensile strength of the glass, the vessel will break.

The broken beakers in my experiment indicated that a flat base resists the compressive forces as the diameter of the vessel shrinks, thereby putting the lowermost part of the vessel in great tension. This makes the object very likely to break. On the other hand, the experiment suggests that a base with a substantial kick can be sufficiently compressed (by bending) to absorb some of the contraction of the walls. Apparently the kicked base bends enough to avoid developing the amount of tension that would break the glass.

3. See, for example, "Medieval Glazed Ware," www.museumoflondon.org.uk/ceramics/pages/ category.asp?cat_name=medieval%20glazed% ware&cat_id=700.

Figure 4
Four unannealed blanks for replicas of an Aldrevandin
beaker made by the author in August 1988.

Therefore, it seems safe to say that, perhaps in addition to the reasons noted above, the purpose of the kick in medieval (and even some later) glass vessels was to reduce the need for precision in the annealing process. In other words, the presence of a kick made it considerably easier to anneal a glass vessel successfully.

If this explanation is correct, it could also help to account for a curious statistical aspect of medieval glass vessels, particularly Merovingian examples (Cabart and Feyeux 1995, p. 11, fig. 1; Feyeux 2003, pp. 241–243, figs. 52–54). Aside from the beakers with kicks in their bases, most of the forms have hemispherical, spheroidal, pointed, or downturned conical bases that are, in effect, "inverse kicks." Preliminary experiments indicate that such forms, like the beakers with kicks, are highly resistant to breakage caused by rapid cooling.

Did some western European glasshouses lose their annealing expertise during the medieval period to such a degree that they began to produce these forms that are so impressively resistant to thermal shock? Glassworkers may well have noticed that undecorated drinking horns and long conical vessels that come to a point or a very narrow diameter at the closed end reliably survive cooling without annealing. It is not unreasonable to suspect that glasshouses may have capitalized on this phenomenon, adapting it to other forms.

In later glasshouse practices, the kick probably survived as a stylized optional feature, divorced from the original reason for which it was created. But during the medieval period, the kick was no doubt functional as well as decorative—and perhaps even essential.

The Soffietta

The *soffietta*[4] is a tool used in glassblowing that consists of a metal cone attached, at its wide end, to a tube. The tube is curved if it is employed by the blower alone and straight if the blower has an assistant (Fig. 5). The worker blows into the tube while pushing the conical part of the tool against the open end of the vessel. The conical shape allows the tool to form an airtight seal with openings of various sizes.

The *soffietta*, which evidently originated sometime during the medieval period, was a major technological advance in the history of glass, and it is arguably one of the most important glassmaking-related inventions after the blowpipe. Previously, the blowpipe had been the only tool with which the worker could inflate molten glass. This was a significant limitation because about half of the time in the glassblowing process is spent with the vessel attached to the pontil, a solid metal rod that is used as a handle. The *soffietta* permitted the worker to complete an object while retaining the option of inflating it further.

Before the invention of the *soffietta*, and even afterward in places where that tool was unknown, all of the shaping that was performed in the later stages of glassblowing had to be accomplished exclusively with hand tools (Figs. 6–10[5]). The process was very straightforward. After the lower half of the vessel was formed, the object was transferred from the blowpipe to the pontil. The upper half of the vessel was reheated and softened in the furnace,

4. The Italian name has been used here, rather than its English equivalent, "puffer," because "*soffietta*" has been widely adopted today by studio glass artists, instructors, and glass historians. In addition, the tool was probably invented in Venice (see page 83). The literal translation of the closely related word *soffietto* is "bellows."

5. For earlier steps in making a similar vessel with this base construction, see Gudenrath 2001, pp. 64–65, figs. 70–78.

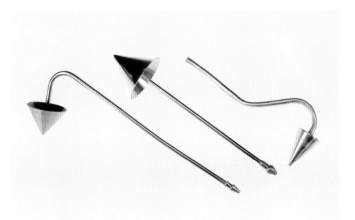

Figure 5
Three *soffietta*s. The two on the left were made by Carlo Dona of Murano, and the one on the right was made by the author.

Forming the Upper Half of a Vessel Using Only Jacks

Figure 6
The lower half of the beaker has been formed (with a base constructed like that of 24), attached to a pontil, and removed from the blowpipe.

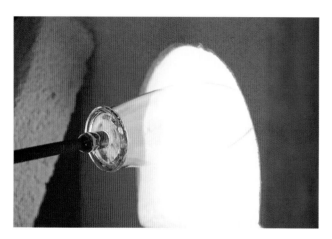

Figure 7
The upper half of the vessel is reheated and softened in the furnace.

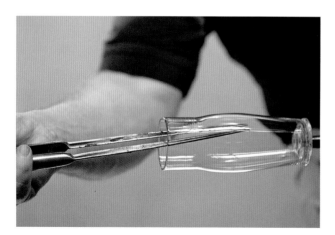

Figure 8
While the pontil is turned, the jacks are used to expand the sides.

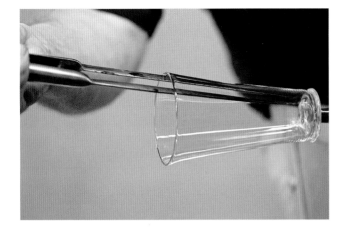

Figure 9
After further reheating, shaping
continues.

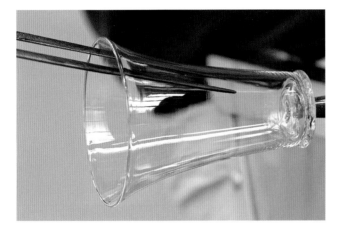

Figure 10
The working cycle of reheating and
shaping continues until the beaker has
been completed. (Tool marks left from
the jacks can be seen covering the interior of the beaker.) The finished object
is removed from the pontil and annealed.

and then the jacks were employed, often forcefully, both to enlarge the opening and to expand and shape the vessel wall. Because contact with the metal tool had the added effect of
cooling the glass rapidly, the work had to be performed quickly, and frequent reheating was
necessary. When the object was completed, it was removed from the pontil and placed in an
annealing oven to be gradually cooled.

Using a *soffietta* in addition to the jacks required more steps that had to be carried out in
a specific order (Figs. 11–18[6]). Here, the jacks were employed almost exclusively to enlarge
the diameter of the opening; the vessel wall was shaped by expansion, entirely with air
pressure provided by means of the *soffietta*. Immediately after the jacks had been used, the
glassblower held the conical part of the *soffietta* against the rim of the vessel while blowing,
often forcefully, into the open end of the attached tube. Between reheatings, this sequence
was repeated until the opening approached its final diameter. Following a last reheating, the

6. See note 2.

Forming the Upper Half of a Vessel Using Jacks and the Soffietta

Figure 11
The lower half of the beaker has been formed (with a kick and a base-ring similar to that of **24**), attached to a pontil, and removed from the blow-pipe.

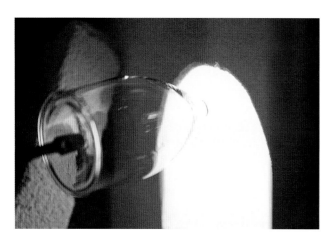

Figure 12
The upper third of the vessel is reheated and softened in the furnace.

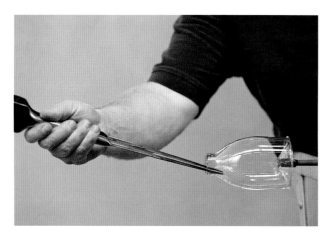

Figure 13
While the pontil is turned, the jacks are used to enlarge the diameter of the opening to about an inch (2.5 cm).

Figure 14
The upper half of the vessel is reheated.

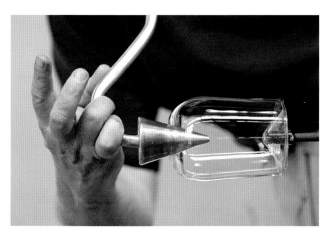

Figure 15
The *soffietta* is used to expand the softened sides by inflation.

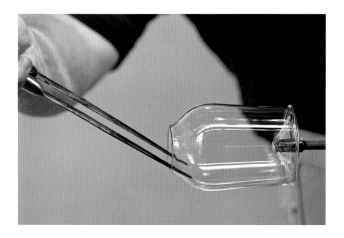

Figure 16
After the upper quarter of the vessel is reheated, the opening is enlarged to a diameter of about two inches (5 cm).

Figure 17
While the glass is still soft, the *soffietta* is employed to further expand the upper quarter of the beaker. (Note that the shaping with the *soffietta* leaves no tool marks on the glass.)

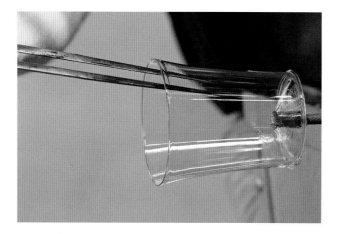

Figure 18
After the upper part is reheated, the jacks are used to give the final shape to the upper eighth or so of the vessel. (Tool marks left by the jacks can be seen only in the immediate vicinity of the rim.) The finished object is removed from the pontil and annealed.

uppermost part of the vessel was given its final shape with the jacks. The object was then annealed.

These two markedly different processes—glassblowing with and without a *soffietta*—leave different marks that can sometimes be detected on historical objects. A glass vessel made without a *soffietta* invariably has extensive tool marks well below its rim. If the upper half of such a vessel was given its final form on the pontil exclusively with jacks, it will have marks on its inner surface. Glassblowing with the help of a *soffietta*, however, is indicated by a very different "footprint." There are few, if any, tool marks in the areas shaped by the *soffietta* because only pressurized air touched the glass. A vessel whose upper half was given its final form in this manner will typically have a heavy concentration of tool marks only in the immediate vicinity of the rim.

Two vessels from the medieval period, one from the Middle East and the other from western Europe, provide excellent illustrations of these differences. A beaker that is believed to have been made in an Islamic workshop in Syria during the 13th century is now in the Hessisches Landesmuseum in Kassel, Germany (see page 47, Figure 13). It is extensively decorated with gilding and enameling. It is one of many examples of its type now in public collections (e.g., **113**).

Upon close inspection, a considerable number of tool marks can be seen on the inner surface of the entire upper half of the beaker. To a limited degree, these marks are also visible in photographs. This beaker and other objects of its type appear to have been shaped exclusively with jacks and without the use of a *soffietta* (Tait 1998; Carboni 2001, pp. 334–335; *Glass of the Sultans* 2001, p. 259).

The well-known Aldrevandin beaker in The British Museum (see page 41) is thought to have been made in Venice in the early 14th century. This name was given to an important group of closely related objccts that consistently reveal a very different working method: they clearly show signs that they were manufactured with the use of a *soffietta* (*Phönix aus Sand und Asche* 1988, pp. 126–160). The exceedingly thin wall of the Aldrevandin beaker has only minimal internal tool marks, except for the uppermost inch (2.5 cm) or so. There, the tool marks are dense and closely spaced. The area below this is mostly unblemished by tool marks because this was the part of the vessel that was shaped using only the *soffietta*.

One of the most striking technical differences between these two groups of beakers is that most Islamic examples have somewhat thick walls, whereas beakers of the Aldrevandin group can be made of glass blown to a paperlike thinness. Apparently, the makers' goals were as different as their means of achieving them.

It appears that, by the early 14th century, Venetian glassworkers were already taking advantage of the *soffietta*. A century later, Angelo Barovier's new *cristallo*, a glass resembling colorless rock crystal, became increasingly important to the growing success of the Venetian glass industry. This was due, in no small measure, to the maestro's ability to work the glass very thinly with complete control. For the master glassblower of Renaissance Venice, the *soffietta* was probably an indispensable tool.

Glass in the Renaissance

Epilogue

BY THE 15th CENTURY, glassmakers in northern Italy and adjoining regions routinely produced thin-walled colorless or almost colorless glass for a variety of uses, from domestic tableware to lamps and apparatus for alchemists.

The glassmakers of late medieval Venice played a prominent role in this industry. Indeed, in the 1400s, Venetian glassmaking already had a centuries-long history. By the eighth or early ninth century, glassworkers were active in the Venetian Lagoon. The first recorded glassmaker in Venice itself is named in a document of 982, after which the names of two glassmakers are found in documents of 1083 and 1090. Evidently the craft flourished because, in 1224, it was recorded that no fewer than 29 glassmakers, who belonged to the Ars Fiolaria (glassblowers' guild) were punished for failing to abide by the rules of the Ufficio di Giustizia, which regulated trade practices. The Venetian government repeatedly asserted control over glassmaking and other industries, and in 1291 it decreed that the glassmakers had to transfer their activities to the nearby island of Murano.

Thereafter, the Venetian glass industry is well documented. We know, for example, that the glassmakers ensured the quality of their products by using raw materials of exceptional purity: quartz pebbles from the Italian mainland and plant ash of superior quality from Egypt and Syria. Indeed, by the early 14th century, the Venetian government required local glass-makers to use Syrian plant ash exclusively. Thus, the unprecedented flowering of Venetian glassmaking in and after the mid-15th century rested on firm local foundations. Surprisingly, however, apart from enameled glasses of the Aldrevandin group (see pages 41–42), few of the products of Venice's late medieval glassmakers have been identified (McCray 1999, pp. 33–65).

Venetian glass of the Renaissance, on the other hand, survives in large quantities, often because spectacular glasses, sometimes made to celebrate a marriage or some other special event, were handed down from one generation to the next as treasured heirlooms. Such objects were sought after all over Europe and were imitated abroad by glassmakers who used the skills pioneered in Venice to make Venetian-style objects that were sometimes adapted to appeal to local taste.

Most high-quality mid-15th-century and later Venetian glass vessels have one or more of the following characteristics: colorless glass of great clarity, glass of brilliant colors that imitated semiprecious stones, gilding and enameling, the extensive use of molds, canes and cane slices, diamond-point engraving, and the assembly of multiple components to make a single object (Whitehouse 2004). These elements were combined with new forms that appealed to a taste for exuberance, opulence, and technical excellence.

Although colorless or almost colorless glass had been made in Italy and adjacent regions since before 1300, it was not until the 15th century that Venetian glassmakers perfected a new colorless glass. They called it *cristallo* because its appearance approximated that of rock crystal. *Cristallo* is not always completely colorless (sometimes it has a faint straw-colored or grayish tinge), and, especially in the 15th century, it was somewhat bubbly. Nevertheless, in the hands of master glassblowers, it could be transformed into objects that ranged from monumental vessels for display to drinking glasses of great fragility.

The Behaim Beaker (**121**) is a fine example of Venetian *cristallo* with meticulous gilded and enameled ornament, made for a foreign patron. The beaker bears the coat of arms of the Behaim family of Nuremberg, Germany. It also has two panels, each containing a single figure: the archangel Michael, shown killing Satan in the form of a dragon, and Saint Catherine of Alexandria, who is depicted next to the wheel on which she was martyred. The unusual combination of Michael and Saint Catherine requires an explanation. It is thought that the beaker was made for the wedding of Michael Behaim and Katerina Lochnerin, the daughter of a rich Nuremberg merchant. The wedding took place on July 7, 1495, and, if the beaker was made for this occasion, it is the earliest precisely datable example of gilded and enameled *cristallo*.

In addition to *cristallo*, Venetian glassmakers created richly colored glasses in imitation of precious and semiprecious stones, such as emeralds. *Calcedonio*, for example, resembles agate, a form of chalcedony characterized by bands of different colors (**122**).

Another feature of Venetian glass made in the Renaissance is the use of molds in greater numbers than were employed by any other European glassmakers since Roman times. Like the Romans, Venetian glassblowers utilized dip molds to decorate parisons (partly inflated bubbles of glass on the end of a blowpipe) with simple, repetitive patterns before they expanded them to their final shapes and sizes; small molds to press or stamp applied motifs, such as the masks and lions' heads that appear on many Venetian and Venetian-style objects (**124**); and full-size molds, made in two parts, to form and decorate an object in a single operation. Sometimes, two or more molds were used in making a single complex object.

The use of canes and cane slices to form overall patterns on blown glass vessels changed the appearance of much Venetian glass. Thin opaque white (and occasionally blue and red) threads were embedded in colorless glass, which was drawn out to make canes with internal patterns. These canes might contain simple stripes or cables of two or more colored plies. Picked up on a *cristallo* parison, they imparted a pattern of stripes or a crisscross netlike decoration to the surface of the vessel. Eighth- and ninth-century glassmakers had produced a small number of vessels decorated with colorless canes containing single or two-ply white or yellow threads (*Phönix aus Sand und Asche* 1988, pp. 69–76, nos. 12–23). No other medieval

Figure 1
Detail of dragon-stem goblet (**127**).

glassmakers employed cane decoration, and its reintroduction and common use became one of the hallmarks of Venetian glass made in and after the Renaissance.

Diamond-point engraving was another Venetian innovation that had no antecedents in medieval Europe. But although finely engraved glasses were produced in 16th-century Venice, ornament of this type was never popular in Italy—in contrast to the Tyrol and countries north of the Alps.

Finally, the glassworkers of Murano mastered the technique of assembling vessels from numerous parts: the 17th-century dragon-stem goblet (**127**), which was made in Venice or at some other place where glasses were created in the Venetian style, contains no fewer than 24 parts, 10 in the dragon itself (Fig. 1).

In a nutshell, between the mid-15th and mid-16th centuries, Venetian glassmakers transformed their late medieval inheritance of techniques, forms, and ornament into something entirely new. They made spectacular progress in melting glasses (such as *calcedonio*) that had never been seen before, they developed a repertoire of innovative forms that appealed to the arbiters of Renaissance taste, and they adorned these forms with rich and sophisticated decoration. These achievements changed the character of luxury glassware all over Europe as, one by one, glassmakers in various parts of Europe began to produce high-quality glassware in the manner of Venice (**125**, **126**, and **128**).

Glass in Ancient Rome: The End of a Tradition

Late Third to Fifth Centuries

1. THE POPULONIA BOTTLE

Italy, late third to early fourth century
H. 18.4 cm, D. (max.) 12.3 cm
Blown; abraded
The Corning Museum of Glass (62.1.31)
Formerly in the collections of Elisa Bonaparte,
*   grand duchess of Tuscany (documented in*
*   1812), and Ray Winfield Smith (591)*

THE BOTTLE was found in a tomb near Piombino, Tuscany, Italy (ancient *Populonia*): hence its name. It is decorated with waterfront scenes and monuments, some of which are identified by inscriptions. The monuments include a triumphal arch surmounted by statues of four horses, a pair of columns supporting statues of gods or humans, and a group of bundles suspended in water. These last features are identified as "OSTRIARIA" (oyster beds),

although they resemble the traditional Italian method of cultivating mussels rather than oysters.

Fewer than a dozen bottles of this type are known. All have the same form and abraded decoration, but they fall into two groups. The Populonia Bottle belongs to the first group, two examples of which are inscribed with the place-name "BAIAE" (modern Baia); the decoration of the bottles in the second group includes an amphitheater, a theater, a temple, and the name "PVTEOLI" (modern Pozzuoli). Pozzuoli, north of Naples in Campania, Italy, was a major Roman port, and nearby Baia was a wealthy seaside resort.

Bibliography
Whitehouse 1997, pp. 270–272, no. 458
(with earlier references).

2. CAGE CUP

Place of manufacture unknown, early fourth century
Cage cup: H. 7.1 cm, D. (rim) 12.2 cm; collar: D. 11 cm;
*   hanger: D. 18.8 cm*
Blown or cast; wheel-cut
The Corning Museum of Glass (87.1.1)

THE TERM "cage cup" is the generic name for Roman objects with openwork decoration. It is generally agreed that late Roman cage cups were made by removing large parts of a thick-walled blank by cutting and grinding the glass with rotating wheels fed with an abrasive slurry, and by using hand tools such as files. Although archeologists have discovered fragments on some relatively humble sites, cage cups are rare, and, in the fourth century, they were luxury items.

The metal collar with three perforated flanges indicates that this cage cup was intended to be suspended. Late Roman and Byzantine descriptions of the interiors of churches and other buildings indicate that some of them were illuminated by hanging lamps. This cage cup, partly filled with olive oil, and with a wick held in place at the center, would have been a spectacular lighting device in a fourth-century church or palace.

Bibliography
Whitehouse 1997, pp. 283–285, no. 478 (with earlier references); *Reflecting Antiquity* 2007, pp. 186–187, no. 81.

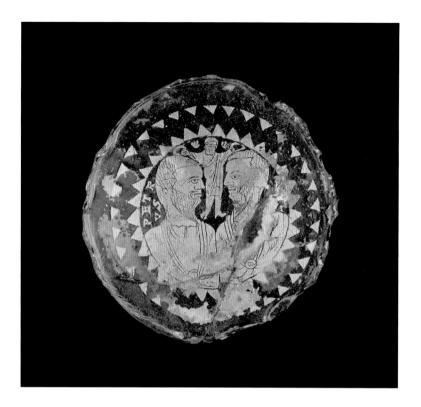

3. GOLD GLASS WITH SAINTS PETER AND PAUL

Probably Rome, fourth century
Max. Dim. 9.2 cm
Blown (two gathers); gold foil applied and incised
The Corning Museum of Glass (62.1.20)
Formerly in the Sangiorgi Collection

THE TWO FIGURES shown in profile are identified by inscriptions as Saints Peter and Paul. The small figure standing between them is Christ, who extends his arms to hold a wreath over the head of each apostle.

The object decorated the bottom of a vessel. The probable method of making the vessel was as follows. The glass that would become the base was blown, and gold foil was applied to the upper surface. The decoration was achieved by removing some of the foil with a stylus and scratching such details as the hair in the apostles' beards. A bubble of glass was inflated and pressed against the decorated surface, creating a "sandwich," with the gold foil protected by two fused layers of glass. After softening the glass by reheating, the glassworker created a vessel of the desired form.

Bibliography
Whitehouse 2001, pp. 248–249, no. 841 (with earlier references); *Picturing the Bible* 2007, p. 192, no. 22.

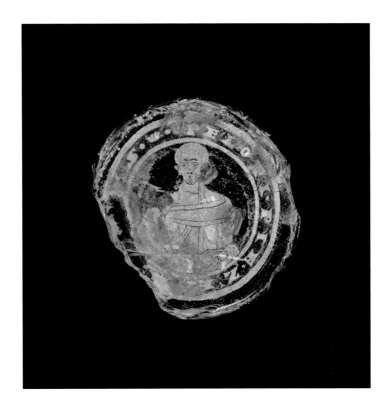

4.   GOLD GLASS WITH PELORIUS

Probably Rome, fourth century
D. 6.2 cm
Blown (two gathers); gold foil applied and incised
The Corning Museum of Glass (54.1.80)
Formerly in the Chalandon and Smith (1071) Collections

THE STANDING FIGURE is identified by the inscription as Pelorius, about whom we know nothing. The complete inscription is ".PELORI. PIE.ZESE[S.VIV]AS." The words may be translated "Pelorius, drink and may you live [for many years]! May you live [for many years]!" "Pie zeses," a Greek phrase adopted by the Romans, was a common toast, as was "Vivas" (may you live!).

For the method of manufacture, see **3**.

The object is said to have been found in Rome.

Bibliography
Whitehouse 2001, p. 248, no. 840 (with earlier references).

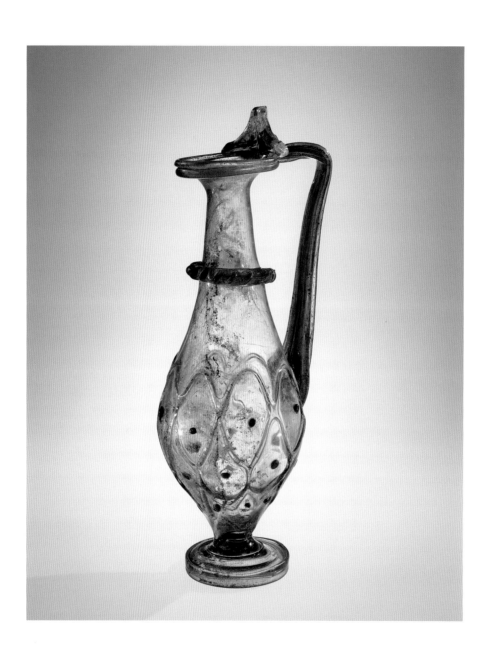

5.   PITCHER

Probably eastern Mediterranean, fourth to fifth century
H. 42.5 cm, D. (rim) 10 cm
Blown; applied
The Corning Museum of Glass (64.1.18)

THE DECORATION on the body was made by applying three horizontal trails, which were pinched together to form a continuous pattern consisting of two rows of diamonds. Each diamond and the spaces between and below the diamonds in the bottom row were embellished with a blob of blue glass. The handle was applied after the trails.

A similar pitcher, also with a pattern of diamonds and blue blobs, said to have come from Kerch in the Crimea, is in the Musée du Louvre, Paris (Eisen 1927, v. 2, p. 441). Another example, with a diamond pattern but no blobs, is in the Israel Museum, Jerusalem (*Dobkin Collection* 2003, p. 188, no. 222). Pitchers with the same form, but no decoration, are in The British Museum, London (*Glass of the Caesars* 1987, p. 147, no. 75); in the State Hermitage Museum, St. Petersburg (Kunina 1997, p. 332, no. 398); and in the possession of the Israel Antiquities Authority (IAA) (*Cradle of Christianity* 2000, p. 84). The pitcher in The British Museum was acquired in Syria, the IAA's specimen was found in the Negev region of Israel, and it is probable that vessels of this type were made in the Levant.

The form of these unusually large pitchers can be matched closely in fourth-century silver vessels (Strong 1966, p. 188).

Bibliography
Glass of the Caesars 1987, p. 148, no. 76 (with earlier references); Whitehouse 2001, pp. 178–179, no. 718 (with earlier references).

6.   HEAD FLASK

Eastern Mediterranean, fourth to fifth century
H. 19.6 cm, D. (rim) 5.7 cm
Mold-blown; applied
The Corning Museum of Glass (59.1.150)
Formerly in the Caruso, Kouchakji, Noorian, and Smith (306) Collections

THE THREE-DIMENSIONAL head was created by blowing a bubble of molten glass into a decorated two-piece mold. Faint vertical ridges behind the ears mark the places where the two parts of the mold came together. The neck was formed outside the mold, and the handle and foot-ring were applied after the flask had been withdrawn from the mold.

The object shares with other vessels the "wishbone" shape of the handle, the coiled foot-ring, and the use of a decorated mold. Most of those vessels have the same deep blue color. They include three identical head flasks (in the Antikenmuseum, Berlin; The J. Paul Getty Museum, Los Angeles; and the collection of Robert and Renée Belfer) and an assortment of beakers, pitchers, and bottles.

This example was once in the collection of the celebrated operatic tenor Enrico Caruso (1873–1921).

Bibliography
Glass of the Caesars 1987, p. 175, no. 96 (with earlier references); Whitehouse 2001, pp. 74–76, no. 548 (with earlier references).

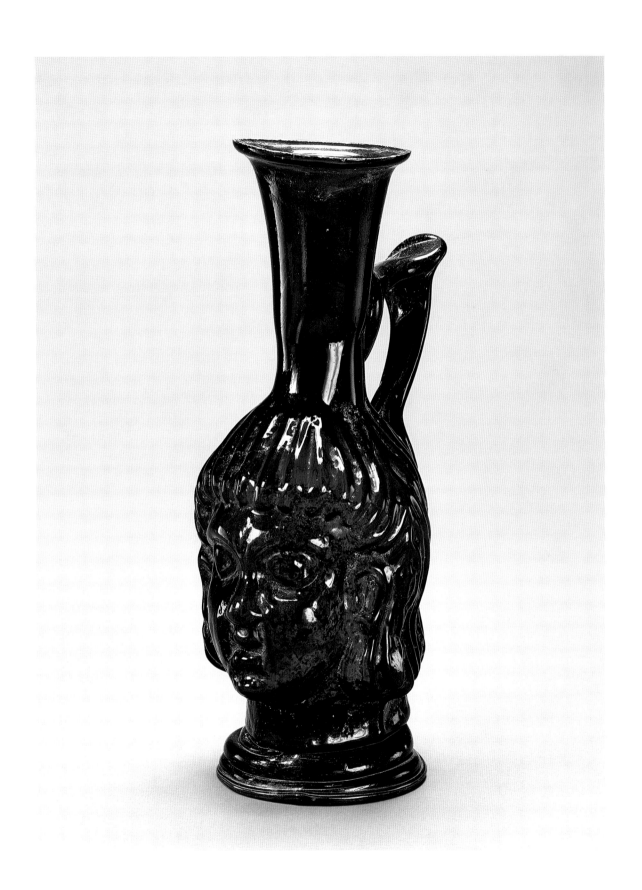

The Early Middle Ages

Fifth to Seventh Centuries

7. PALM CUP

Rhineland, Low Countries, or northern France, seventh century
H. 4.8 cm, D. 12 cm
Blown; applied
The Corning Museum of Glass (54.1.93)
Formerly in the collections of Armand Baar, Liège, Belgium,
 and Ray Winfield Smith (763)

PALM CUPS are shallow drinking vessels with a rounded base that fits in the palm of the hand. They were widely used in the early Middle Ages, and examples have been found in Germany, the Low Countries, France, and the United Kingdom. This example was decorated with two spirally wound trails. One trail was wound seven times around the top of the vessel and rolled on a smooth, flat surface until it was flush with the wall. The other trail was wound six times around the lower wall.

Some palm cups were decorated by inflating the bubble of glass in a mold.

Palm cups of this type were in use between about 600 and 650 or somewhat later.

This cup is said to have been found at Péronne in the Somme department of northern France.

Bibliography
Whitehouse 2001, pp. 142–143, no. 652 (with earlier references).

8. PALM CUP WITH INSCRIPTION

Northern France, seventh century
H. 9.6 cm, D. 8.5 cm
Blown in mold with two vertical sections
The Metropolitan Museum of Art, New York (17.191.360,
*   gift of J. Pierpont Morgan)*

A SMALL NUMBER of the Merovingian glass vessels that were blown in dip molds have inscriptions in low relief. This example belongs to a group of six related palm cups, blown in molds with two vertical sections, that are datable to the seventh century and were probably made in the Marne or Aube departments of northern France. It has an inscription on the lower wall and a cross on the bottom. The inscriptions on all six cups are similar, but not identical; evidently they were blown in six different molds. None of the inscriptions has been deciphered. Indeed, while some of the letters are legible, others are so badly formed that Rademacher (1942, p. 305) concluded that the "inscriptions" are unreadable and have a purely decorative function.

Bibliography
Cabart 1993, p. 228.

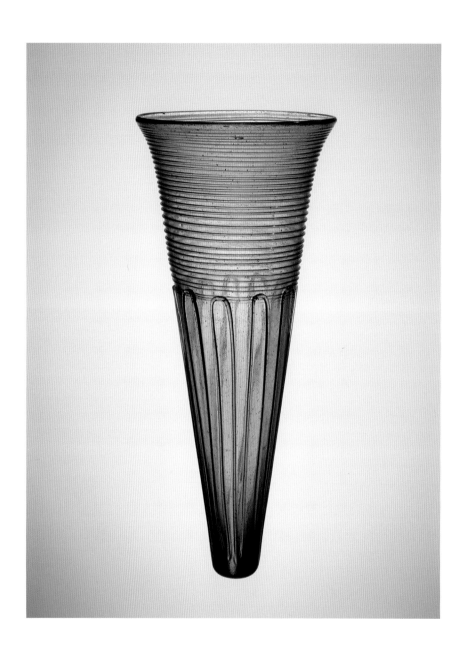

9. CONE BEAKER

England, the Low Countries, northern France, or Germany,
*   mid-fifth to sixth century*
H. 23.2 cm, D. (rim) 9.9 cm
Blown; applied
The Corning Museum of Glass (66.1.247)

BEAKERS with horizontal trails and vertical loops are known as the "Kempston" type, after the find-place in the eastern United Kingdom of a particularly fine example. Kempston beakers from datable archeological contexts include fifth-century specimens from Alfriston, Mitcham, and Guildown in the United Kingdom, and Huy/St.-Victor in Belgium. Other vessels have been found in sixth-century graves at Alfriston and Dover in the United Kingdom, and Baisy-Thy in Belgium.

This beaker is said to have been found at Acklam, now a suburb of Middlesborough in Yorkshire, United Kingdom, in 1892.

Bibliography
Whitehouse 2001, pp. 149–150, no. 667 (with earlier references).

10. CONE BEAKER

England, perhaps Faversham, seventh century
H. 17.6 cm, D. (rim) 8.5 cm
Blown; applied
The Corning Museum of Glass (85.1.4)

THE BEAKER was found in 1862 in The King's Field at Faversham, Kent. This is the site of an Anglo-Saxon cemetery, discovered during railroad construction in 1858, which contained several hundred graves of the sixth and seventh centuries. Many of the objects that accompanied burials in the cemetery passed into the Gibbs Collection and then to The British Museum, London.

This beaker is illustrated in a watercolor signed "Wm. Webster Hoare" and annotated by William P. Hoare, both on February 2, 1878. The former owner, P. T. Cooke, supplied the following information: William Palmer Hoare, his great-grandfather, was a physician at Faversham from 1838 to 1865; William Webster Hoare was Cooke's great-uncle. After the death of Dr. Hoare, members of the family (including Cooke's mother) immigrated to Australia, taking the beaker with them. It remained in the family until 1985.

Only one other beaker of this type is known. It, too, was found in The King's Field. Faversham was probably the site of a vill of the kings of Kent, and it is thought that some of the glass from The King's Field (including the two beakers) was made locally.

Bibliography
Whitehouse 1986; Whitehouse 2001, pp. 151–153, no. 668.

11. BELL BEAKER

Probably Germany, the Low Countries, or France, sixth century
H. (surviving) 15 cm, D. 8 cm
Mold-blown; applied
The Corning Museum of Glass (62.1.7)

BELL BEAKERS (German, *Sturzbecher*) are so called because they are shaped like an inverted bell. The earliest bell beakers were made before about 500, and the type remained in use throughout the sixth century.

The spiraling ribs of this tall bell beaker were made by blowing the bubble of molten glass into a dip mold with vertical ribs, withdrawing it, and, while twirling the bubble, inflating it to the desired shape and size.

The beaker has been compared with a vessel of similar shape in the National Museum, Tokyo, with a molded rooster on the base. The rooster is in "pure Sasanian style": hence the suggestion that this object may have been made in Iran (*Royal Hunter* 1978, p. 158, no. 81). However, although bright green glass was uncommon in the Merovingian world, it seems probable that the object is European.

Bibliography
Whitehouse 2001, pp. 153–154, no. 670.

12. BELL BEAKER

Germany, the Low Countries, or France, fifth to sixth century
H. (surviving) 10.5 cm, D. 6.9–7.4 cm
Blown; applied
The Corning Museum of Glass (63.1.9)

BELL BEAKERS are among the most common Merovingian glass drinking vessels in continental Europe. This example belongs to group V.a.ii in the classification by Harden (1956) and to type 52 according to the scheme devised by Feyeux (1995). The body of the beaker is complete, but a knob is missing from the bottom.

The decoration was made by winding a trail of white glass around the bubble of molten glass and dragging it up to form a series of swags. The bubble was then marvered, softened by reheating, and blown to its final shape and size.

Bibliography
Whitehouse 2001, pp. 213–214, no. 779.

13. BELL BEAKER

Germany, the Low Countries, or France,
  fifth to early sixth century
H. (surviving) 7.9 cm, D. 7.9 cm
Blown; applied
The Corning Museum of Glass
  (79.1.167, bequest of Jerome Strauss)
Formerly in the Strauss Collection (S2655)

BELL BEAKERS were widely used in western Europe in the fifth and early sixth centuries. The presence of opaque white trails is sometimes said to indicate a relatively early date. Beakers of this type belong to group V.a.ii in the classification by Donald B. Harden.

Bibliography
Whitehouse 2001, p. 154, no. 671.

14. CLAW BEAKER

Germany, fifth to sixth century
H. 18.7 cm, D. 10.8 cm
Blown; applied
The Metropolitan Museum of Art, New York
* (81.10.189, gift of Henry G. Marquand)*

CLAW BEAKERS are among the most distinctive early medieval glass vessels. After the body of the beaker had been formed on the blowpipe, two trails were applied to the wall and wound spirally around its upper and lower sections, leaving an undecorated zone in the middle. Next, two horizontal rows of claws were applied to the midsection and lower wall, using the technique described on page 27.

Finally, the vessel was transferred from the blowpipe to the pontil in order to finish the rim.

According to the museum's records, the beaker was found in "Bellenberg Voehringen." Bellenberg and Vöhringen are two municipalities, just a few kilometers apart, in the Neu-Ulm district of Bavaria, southern Germany.

15. BOTTLE USED AS A RELIQUARY

*Place of manufacture uncertain, probably
  seventh to eighth century*
H. 7.5 cm, D. (max.) 5.5 cm
Blown; engraved
*The Metropolitan Museum of Art, New York
  (81.10.268, gift of Henry G. Marquand, 1881)*

THE ENGRAVING on the bottle shows that it was used as a reliquary. In addition to birds and a martyr's wreath, there are two inscriptions. The first inscription names Saint Ursula, and the second ("XI.M.V") seems to refer to the virgins who, according to legend, were martyred with her in Cologne, Germany.

An inscription, probably of the fifth century, in the Church of Saint Ursula at Cologne records the rebuilding of a ruined basilica in honor of virgins who had suffered martyrdom on that spot. The inscription does not record the names or number of the martyrs. Ninth-century and later liturgical texts do supply such information, but they are inconsistent. Ursula ranks first in one of these sources. The number 11,000 (*undecim millia* in Latin) was introduced around the year 900. Various explanations have been suggested: that it derived from a personal name (Undecimillia or Ximillia) or from the abbreviation XI.M.V (*undecim martyres virgines*, "eleven virgin martyrs"), which was mistakenly thought to stand for *undecim millia virgines*.

16. BOTTLE

Probably Low Countries or northern France,
*   probably fourth to mid-sixth century*
H. 28.1 cm, D. (rim) 4.5 cm
Blown (body blown in full-size mold)
The Corning Museum of Glass (54.1.97)

THE OBJECT is believed to be Merovingian, although it is not typical of bottles of this period, most of which were blown either offhand or in ribbed dip molds. An alternative possibility is that the object was made in the late Roman period.

A change in the weathering, about 10 centimeters above the bottom, suggests that the object stood upright (presumably in a tomb), partly covered in earth or at least occasionally submerged in water.

Bibliography
Whitehouse 1997, pp. 181–182, no. 320.

The Central Middle Ages

Eighth to 11th Centuries

17. FUNNEL BEAKER

Western Europe, 10th century
H. 15.3 cm, D. (rim) 10.9 cm
Blown; applied
Statens Historiska Museum, Stockholm (SHM 34000: Bj 577)

FUNNEL BEAKERS were later versions of early medieval cone beakers such as **9** and **10**. They were made in western Europe in the ninth and 10th centuries. An example is illustrated in a 10th-century manuscript of the Martyrology of Saint Wandalbert (d. about 870) in the Biblioteca Apostolica Vaticana (see page 29, Figure 1).

The beaker was found in Grave 577 at Birka, on the island of Björkö in Lake Mälaren, 30 kilometers west of Stockholm, Sweden. Birka was a major trading center between the mideighth century and about 960. Although Birka was the site of the first Christian church in Sweden, established as a result of diplomatic contacts between the king of Sweden and Emperor Louis the Pious in 829, most of its inhabitants were pagans, and they buried useful objects with their dead.

Bibliography
Arbman 1940–43, v. 1, p. 161, and v. 2, pl. 190.1.

18. "LINEN SMOOTHER"

Place of manufacture uncertain, eighth to 11th century
H. 3.8 cm, D. 6 cm
Pressed in mold (?)
The Corning Museum of Glass (59.1.291)
Formerly in the collection of Ray Winfield Smith (152)

"LINEN SMOOTHERS" have been found in many parts of Europe, from Scandinavia to Italy, and they were made between the eighth and 11th centuries (Macquet 1990). All are circular, and they vary in diameter between about six and nine centimeters. One surface is smooth and convex, while the other surface may be uneven. The smoother usually has a pontil mark, which shows that the object was held on a metal rod while it was shaped. This demonstrates that linen smoothers were made for a purpose and are not, as some have supposed, unused glass from the bottoms of crucibles. The rounded surface suggests that the objects were used for smoothing something: textiles or clothing, or possibly animal skins that were to become the pages of handwritten books. They may, however, have been employed in the preparation of food.

Bibliography
Glass from the Ancient World 1957, p. 219, no. 441.

Late Medieval Glass

12th to 15th Centuries

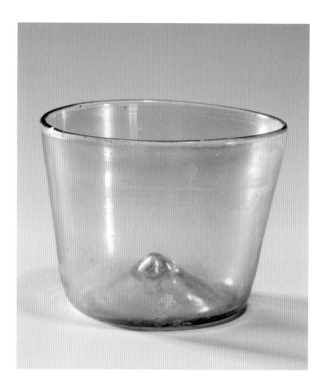

19. BEAKER

Perhaps southern Germany, 14th to 15th century
H. 5.4 cm, D. 7.1 cm
Blown
Diözesanmuseum Freising (28)

UNDECORATED BEAKERS with a truncated conical form and a prominent kick were widely used and enjoyed a long life in late-medieval Germany and adjoining regions. A fragmentary example found during excavations at Mainz, Germany, dates from the late 13th or 14th century (*Phönix aus Sand und Asche* 1988, p. 230, no. 221), while similar objects from the Palazzo Vitelleschi at Tarquinia, Italy, belong to the late 14th century (Newby 1999, pp. 52–53). This example was probably found in the diocese of Freising, Germany, but the exact find-place is unknown.

Bibliography
Phönix aus Sand und Asche 1988, p. 288, no. 325.

20. BEAKER

Germany, 15th century
H. 7.5 cm, D. (rim) 8.5 cm
Blown (in dip mold)
Museum für Angewandte Kunst Frankfurt,
  Frankfurt am Main (13410)
Formerly in the Pfoh Collection

TRUNCATED CONICAL beakers, like **19**, are also found with overall patterns of mold-blown decoration; indeed, they were produced in great numbers in green forest glass (**64–66** and **68–69**), as well as in France (*A travers le verre* 1989, pp. 223–225, nos. 181–187), Italy (Newby 1999, pp. 53–65), and elsewhere.

This example is unusual in its combination of almost colorless glass, mold-blown ribs, and a deep blue trail around the rim (for other colorless vessels with blue trails on the rim, see **31** and **38–42**).

Bibliography
Phönix aus Sand und Asche 1988, pp. 308–309, no. 361.

21. BEAKER DECORATED WITH PRUNTS

Europe, 13th century, or Western Asia, 10th to 11th century
H. 10.7 cm, D. (rim) 6.9 cm
Blown; applied
Glasmuseum Hentrich, Museum Kunst Palast, Düsseldorf (P 1980-1)

PRUNTED BEAKERS of various shapes and sizes came into use in parts of central and southern Europe in the 13th century. It is widely believed that European glassmakers were inspired by beakers made in the Islamic Near and Middle East. Beakers decorated with (usually small) prunts have been excavated at Hama, Syria (Riis and Poulsen 1957, pp. 54–61, figs. 157–162), and other sites in Western Asia, but the relationship, if such exists, between the Islamic and European objects remains to be determined. This example, of unknown provenance, has been identified as an Islamic beaker of the 10th or 11th century, possibly from Nishapur in northeastern Iran, but it may well be European.

Bibliography
Phönix aus Sand und Asche 1988, p. 194, no. 166 (with earlier references).

22. BEAKER DECORATED WITH PRUNTS

Northern Italy, Switzerland, or southern Germany, 13th to 14th century
H. 12.5 cm, D. (rim) 8.4 cm
Blown; applied
The Corning Museum of Glass (87.3.33)
Formerly in the collection of Fritz Biemann

IN THE LATE 1930s, excavations at Corinth in southern Greece brought to light the remains of a medieval glass factory. Among the most distinctive products were prunted beakers. Numerous coins from the site suggested that the factory operated in the first half of the 12th century, when Greece was part of the Byzantine Empire. Corinth was attacked by Normans from Sicily in 1147, and for 50 years it was believed that the glassmakers were transported to that island. There, it was supposed, they made prunted beakers, which were imitated in Italy and north of the Alps. New evidence for the date of the factory, however, shows that this assumption is false. Indeed, today it appears probable that the prunted beakers at Corinth were made by glassmakers from Italy around the year 1300.

Bibliography
Mille anni 1982, pp. 68–69, no. 48; "Recent Important Acquisitions," *JGS*, v. 24, 1982, p. 91, no. 14; *Phönix aus Sand und Asche* 1988, pp. 200–201, no. 178; Stiaffini 1999, p. 94, fig. 78.

23. BEAKER DECORATED WITH PRUNTS

Germany, Switzerland, or Italy, 13th to early 14th century
H. 10.7 cm, D. (rim) 8.7 cm
Blown; applied
Collection of Karl Amendt, Krefeld (LP 2010-4)

See **21** and **22**.
This object is believed to have been found in Speyer, Germany.

Bibliography
Amendt Collection 1987, pp. 36–37, no. 4; *Phönix aus Sand und Asche* 1988, p. 195, no. 168; *Amendt Collection* 2005, p. 68, no. 4.

24. BEAKER DECORATED WITH PRUNTS

Germany or an adjoining region to the south or east,
*   13th to 14th century*
H. 9.3 cm, D. (rim) 8 cm
Blown; applied
The Corning Museum of Glass (2009.3.50)

PRUNTED BEAKERS were among the most common types of glass drinking vessels used in Germany, parts of central Europe, Switzerland, and Italy in the later Middle Ages (*Phönix aus Sand und Asche* 1988, pp. 192–217, nos. 166–204). The glass workshop at Corinth, Greece, which produced prunted beakers and was once believed to date to the 11th to 12th centuries, is now thought to have been operated by Italians between the late 13th and early 14th centuries (Whitehouse 1991, 1993). The relationship between European prunted beakers and prunted vessels made in Syria remains to be clarified, but prunted beakers from sites in the Crimea (e.g., **46** and **47**) are now thought to be imports from Italy rather than local products.

25. BEAKER DECORATED WITH PRUNTS

Germany, late 13th to 14th century
H. 9 cm, D. (rim) 7.5 cm
Blown; applied
Collection of Karl Amendt, Krefeld (LP 2010-25)

THIS TRANSPARENT pale blue beaker is decorated with six horizontal rows of rather irregular prunts. Those in the second row from the top, for example, are noticeably smaller than those in the third and fourth rows.

The beaker is reported to have been found in the vicinity of Mainz or Speyer, Germany.

Bibliography
Amendt Collection 1987, p. 48, no. 18.

26. BEAKER DECORATED WITH PRUNTS

Germany or Switzerland, late 13th to 14th century
H. 11.2 cm, D. (rim) 12.4 cm
Blown; applied
Museum zu Allerheiligen, Schaffhausen (6285)

THE BEAKER is decorated with six rather irregular rows, each containing seven prunts. As on other beakers from Schaffhausen (including **27** and *Phönix aus Sand und Asche* 1988, p. 213, no. 194), the prunts are small and were detached from the wall of the vessel with a twisting motion that produced an appearance not unlike that of a snail shell.

Bibliography
Phönix aus Sand und Asche 1988, p. 213, no. 192.

27. BEAKER DECORATED WITH PRUNTS

Germany or Switzerland, late 13th to 14th century
H. 7.1 cm, D. (rim) 8.7 cm
Blown; applied
Museum zu Allerheiligen, Schaffhausen (6287)

THIS SMALL beaker is decorated with six horizontal rows, each containing eight small prunts. Like **26**, but unlike the majority of prunted beakers, it has a rim diameter greater than its height. For other prunted beakers with similar proportions, see *Amendt Collection* 1987, p. 49, nos. 22–24; and *Amendt Collection* 2005, pp. 88–90, nos. 26–31.

27, like **26**, was found in a medieval latrine in the Benedictine Kloster zu Allerheiligen in Schaffhausen, Switzerland, in 1921.

Bibliography
Phönix aus Sand und Asche 1988, p. 213, no. 193.

28. BEAKER DECORATED WITH PRUNTS

Germany or Switzerland, late 13th to 14th century
H. 7.1 cm, D. (rim) 6.6 cm
Blown; applied
LVR-Landesmuseum Bonn (68.0483)
Formerly in the Bremen Collection

THIS BEAKER is decorated with six horizontal rows of pointed prunts between a continuous horizontal trail at the bottom of the rim and a "toed" trail at the junction of the wall and the base.

Bibliography
Phönix aus Sand und Asche 1988, p. 214, no. 197.

29. BEAKER DECORATED WITH PRUNTS

Germany, 14th century
H. 7.1 cm, D. (rim) 5.2 cm
Blown; applied
Collection of Karl Amendt, Krefeld (LP 2010-32)

THE GLOBULAR form of this beaker is un-usual, as is the care with which the rim was finished. A single narrow trail was applied to the wall of the vessel, just below the rim. A second trail was applied to the bottom of the wall and pinched into a row of "toes." The area between the two trails is filled with six rather irregular horizontal rows of prunts.

The beaker is said to have been found in the vicinity of Mainz or Speyer, Germany.

Bibliography
Amendt Collection 1987, pp. 51–52, no. 25; *Phönix aus Sand und Asche* 1988, p. 216, no. 201; *Amendt Collection* 2005, p. 91, no. 32.

30. BOTTLE

Probably northern Italy, 14th to 15th century
H. 22.7 cm, D. (max.) 12.6 cm
Gather inflated in dip mold, withdrawn,
    and blown to final shape and size
The Corning Museum of Glass (89.3.12, gift,
    funds from Alberta Stout)

THIS BOTTLE was found at Ravenna in Emilia-Romagna, northern Italy. Similar bottles, with or without a bulge near the top of the neck, are depicted in Italian paintings of the 14th and 15th centuries. They are shown in various contexts. In pictures of the Last Supper, the Wedding at Cana, and Herod's Feast, they often appear filled with wine, together with pattern-molded or prunted beakers. Very few examples survive intact, although numerous fragments have been found in archeological excavations. The word *inghistere* (the spelling varies) in Venetian and other medieval documents probably refers to bottles of this type.

Bibliography
"Recent Important Acquisitions," *JGS*, v. 32, 1990, p. 190, no. 3.

31. DISH WITH APPLIED DECORATION

Probably Germany, about 1250–1350
H. 7.4 cm, D. (rim) 25.6 cm
Blown; applied
Glasmuseum Hentrich, Museum Kunst Palast,
   Düsseldorf (P 1985-297)

DISHES of this form and with similar decoration made by applying bright blue trails have a wide distribution in Europe, and it is not yet clear where all of them were made. In addition to finds from Germany (including Mainz or Speyer, and Freiburg) and adjoining regions (such as Strasbourg), examples have been found at sites in southern France (including the glass workshop at La Seube near Montpellier: Foy 1985, p. 48, fig. 34; *A travers le verre* 1989, pp. 81 and 234–237, nos. 209–215). Fragments of similar vessels from sites in the United Kingdom may be imports from southern France (Tyson 2000, pp. 107–109, nos. g222–g233).

Bibliography
Phönix aus Sand und Asche 1988, pp. 283–284, no. 319.

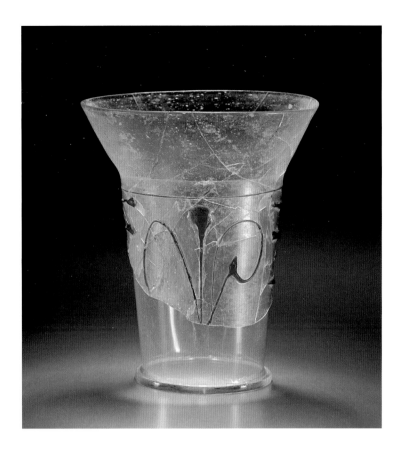

32. BEAKER WITH APPLIED DECORATION

Probably Germany, second half of the 13th century
*   to early 14th century*
H. (surviving) 8.9 cm, D. (rim) 9.8 cm
Blown; applied
Collection of Karl Amendt, Krefeld (LP 2010-5)

IT WAS a common practice to decorate color-less or almost colorless glass vessels with deep blue trails, and examples have been recovered from late medieval contexts in Italy, Switzer-land, Germany, France, and adjoining regions. The decoration of this beaker, however, appears to be unique. It consists of two motifs resembling simplified fleurs-de-lis separated by abstract patterns.

The object, of which only the upper part survives, was probably found in Worms, Germany.

Bibliography
Amendt Collection 1987, p. 38, no. 5; *Phönix aus Sand und Asche* 1988, p. 189, no. 160.

33. BEAKER WITH APPLIED DECORATION

Probably Germany, late 13th to early 14th century
H. 15 cm, D. (rim) 11.2 cm
Blown; applied
Museum für Angewandte Kunst Frankfurt, Frankfurt am Main (13423)
Formerly in the Pfoh Collection

THIS BEAKER of almost colorless glass is decorated with horizontal trails of colorless and dark blue glass, which extend from the top of the wall to the base. The trails on the wall are plain blue at the top and the bottom, separated by five more or less equally spaced trails, three of which are pinched to form a series of short, vertical ridges; the edge of the base has a pinched colorless trail. Fragments of a similar colorless and blue beaker, found at Breisach, Baden-Württemberg, in 1980, are in the Landesmuseum Württemberg, Stuttgart (*Phönix aus Sand und Asche* 1988, p. 183, no. 151).

Bibliography
Phönix aus Sand und Asche 1988, p. 182, no. 149.

34. BEAKER WITH APPLIED DECORATION

Probably Germany, late 13th to early 14th century
H. 10.3 cm, D. (rim) 9 cm
Blown; applied
Glasmuseum Hentrich, Museum Kunst Palast,
  Düsseldorf (1940-59)
Formerly in the Miller von Aichholz
  and Jantzen Collections

See **33**.

Bibliography
Phönix aus Sand und Asche 1988, p. 182, no. 150
(with earlier references).

35. BEAKER WITH APPLIED DECORATION

Probably Germany, late 13th to early 14th century
H. 10.1 cm, D. (rim) 8.1–8.3 cm
Blown; applied
The Corning Museum of Glass (2009.3.49)

THE ALTERNATING ROWS of plain blue and pinched colorless trails are characteristic of a group of beakers made in Germany and perhaps also adjoining regions in the late 13th and early 14th centuries (*Phönix aus Sand und Asche* 1988, pp. 180–183, nos. 150–152). A similar but smaller beaker, with alternating rows of plain and pinched trails, all of the same color as the beaker itself, may have been found in London; if so, presumably it was imported from the Continent (*ibid.*, pp. 183–184, no. 153). Another beaker of this type (**48**) was found near Novorossiysk in the Caucasus.

36. BEAKER WITH APPLIED DECORATION

Germany, late 14th century
H. 7.4 cm, D. (rim) 7.1 cm
Blown; applied
Museum für Angewandte Kunst Frankfurt,
    Frankfurt am Main (13417)
Formerly in the Pfoh Collection

A SIMILAR BEAKER was discovered in the chapel at Bandekow in the Hagenow district of Mecklenburg–West Pomerania, Germany, in 1862. Its wax cover bears the seal of Bishop Detlev von Parkentin, who occupied the see of Ratzeburg from 1395 to 1419 (see below).

Bibliography
Phönix aus Sand und Asche 1988, p. 183, no. 152.

37. BEAKER WITH APPLIED DECORATION

Probably Germany, about 1250–1350
H. 10.1 cm, D. (rim) 9.8 cm
Blown; applied
Glasmuseum Hentrich, Museum Kunst Palast, Düsseldorf (1979-7)

THIS OBJECT, which was probably found at Speyer, Germany, belongs to a small group of beakers with very distinctive ornament, consisting of alternating colorless and deep blue vertical trails that extend from the top to the bottom of the wall. Each trail is overlaid by a second trail applied as a series of tiny loops. The overall effect is one of careful, almost miniature decoration. Other beakers of this type have been found at Schaffhausen, Switzerland; Regensburg, Germany; and Strasbourg, northeastern France (*Phönix aus Sand und Asche* 1988, pp. 186–187, nos. 156–158).

Bibliography
Phönix aus Sand und Asche 1988, p. 186, no. 155 (with earlier references).

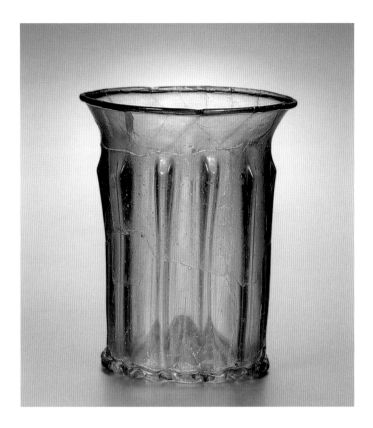

38. BEAKER WITH VERTICAL RIBS

Probably Germany, second half of the 13th century
or early 14th century
H. 10.2 cm, D. (rim) 8.4 cm
Blown; applied
Collection of Karl Amendt, Krefeld (LP 2010-9)

BEAKERS with mold-blown vertical ribs have a wide distribution, extending from Lübeck, Germany, in the north (*Phönix aus Sand und Asche* 1988, pp. 222–223, nos. 210 and 211) and Strasbourg, France, in the west (*ibid*., pp. 221–222, no. 209) to Corinth, Greece, in the south and the east (Davidson 1952, p. 114, no. 746). Most reported find-places, however, are in southern Germany, Switzerland, and Italy, with outliers in Bosnia and Herzegovina, and Kosovo (Kojić and Wenzel 1967, figs. 3 and 9;

Križanac 2001, p. 18, no. 69). One fragmentary beaker was recovered from a 14th-century embankment in the Venetian Lagoon (Zecchin 1987–90, v. 1, p. 7, bottom right), and it is possible that the vessels from the Balkans were exported from Venice.

This example is thought to have been found in Mainz, Germany.

Bibliography
Amendt Collection 2005, pp. 71 and 247, no. 9.

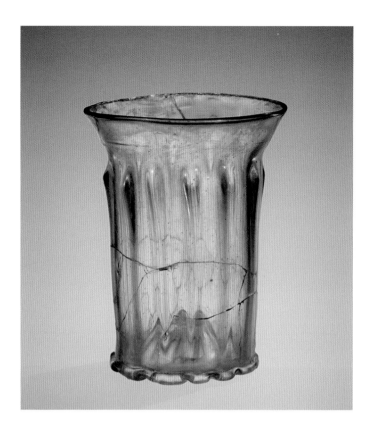

39. BEAKER WITH VERTICAL RIBS

Probably Germany, second half of the 13th century
*   or early 14th century*
H. 9.5 cm, D. (rim) 7.6 cm
Blown; applied
The Corning Museum of Glass (88.3.47)

THIS OBJECT, like the similar beakers (**38** and **40**) and the beaker or *Scheuer* (**41**), has a combination of colorless glass, vertical ribs, and a deep blue lip wrap. All three objects are thought to have been made in southern Germany, although examples have been found in northern Germany, eastern France, the Balkans, and Greece (see page 141).

Bibliography
"Recent Important Acquisitions," *JGS*, v. 31, 1989, p. 103, no. 8.

40. BEAKER WITH VERTICAL RIBS

*Probably Germany, second half of the 13th century
  or early 14th century*
H. 9.5 cm, D. (rim) 8 cm
Blown; applied
LVR-Landesmuseum Bonn (68.0563)
Formerly in the Bremen Collection

THIS BEAKER, together with **38** and **39**, forms part of a group of very similar objects with a deep blue lip wrap, vertical ribs, and a "toed" base. They have a wide distribution that extends from eastern France to the Balkans and Greece. However, the similarity of the beakers may suggest that they were made in a small number of closely related workshops.

Bibliography
Phönix aus Sand und Asche 1988, p. 220, no. 205.

41. BEAKER OR *SCHEUER* WITH VERTICAL RIBS

Probably Germany, second half of the 13th century
*   or early 14th century*
H. 6.6 cm, D. (rim) 5.1 cm
Blown; applied
Collection of Karl Amendt, Krefeld (LP 2010-10)

THE SHAPE of this unusual vessel resembles that of a *Scheuer* (such as **42**, **87**, **88**, and **109**), although it lacks the horizontal handle that is characteristic of the latter. Similar beakers have been found at Nottuln (near Münster) and Nuremberg, both in Germany.

The combination of colorless glass and a bright blue lip wrap or trailed decoration is found on several types of vessels (including **38** and **39**) that were made in southern Germany, Switzerland, and northern Italy in the second half of the 13th century and the early 14th century.

The find-place of this object is unknown.

Bibliography
Amendt Collection 1987, p. 40, no. 8; Amendt Collection 2005, pp. 72 and 248, no. 10.

42. SCHEUER

Perhaps Germany, probably 13th to 14th century
H. 6.6 cm, D. (rim) 6.3 cm
Blown; applied
Landesmuseum Württemberg, Stuttgart (G.11.124)
Formerly in the Lanna Collection

THE GERMAN WORD *Scheuer* refers to a drinking vessel with a short cylindrical neck, a biconical or hemispherical body, and a single handle that projects out and up from the mid-point of the wall.

The place of manufacture and date of this *Scheuer* are uncertain because no close parallels are known. The combination of almost colorless and deep blue glass suggests comparison with glasses made between about 1250 and 1350, like the dish (**31**), beakers (**32–40**), and *Scheuer* or *Scheuer*-like vessel (**41**). On the other hand, the shape of the handle resembles that of late 15th- to mid-16th-century objects, such as **87–89** and **109**. The solution to the problem of the date of this vessel is most likely to come from finding similar objects in datable archeological contexts.

Bibliography
Phönix aus Sand und Asche 1988, pp. 235–236, no. 229.

43. *KRAUTSTRUNK*

Germany, late 15th to early 16th century
H. 6.6 cm, D. (rim) 7.5 cm
Blown; applied
Diözesanmuseum Freising (P 851-19)

SMALL *Krautstrünke* (beakers decorated with prunts) of this type were made in Bavaria and Bohemia toward the end of the 15th century and in the early decades of the 16th century. For a similar beaker in the Bayerisches Nationalmuseum in Munich, see Rückert 1982, v. 1, p. 44, no. 9.

The glass is almost colorless. Its surface has a cloudy appearance because the glass has begun to crizzle (that is, moisture has leached some of the alkaline component from the outermost part of the glass, with the result that the surface has deteriorated). The object is unusual because almost all *Krautstrünke* were made of transparent green forest glass (see page 44).

This example was found in the diocese of Freising, Germany, although the exact findplace is not recorded.

Bibliography
Phönix aus Sand und Asche 1988, pp. 342–343, no. 413.

44. GOBLET

Western Germany, the Low Countries, or northern France,
*   13th to 14th century*
H. (surviving) 21.5 cm, D. (rim) 4.4 cm
Blown (bowl blown in dip mold); applied
Collection of Karl Amendt, Krefeld (LP 2010-18)

GOBLETS with ribbed bowls, narrow stems, and bell- or trumpet-shaped feet were made in the Low Countries, northern France, and the westernmost parts of Germany from the late 13th century. Most examples have shallow, truncated conical bowls with pinched vertical ribs on the lower wall. A much smaller number of goblets, including this example, have tulip-shaped bowls decorated by inflating the bubble of molten glass in a dip mold. The most famous goblet with a tulip-shaped bowl had been concealed in the masonry of the church of the Augustinians at Rouen in the Haute-Normandie region of northwestern France in the 14th century, and it was discovered when the ruined church was demolished in 1949.

This example was found in the middle Rhineland.

Bibliography
Amendt Collection 1987, pp. 42–43, no. 13; *Amendt Collection* 2005, pp. 79 and 250, no. 18.

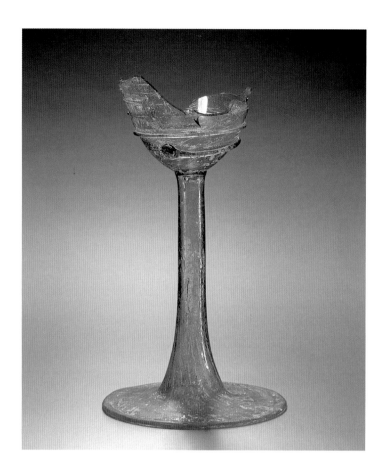

45. GOBLET WITH HOLLOW STEM

Southern Netherlands or northern France, perhaps 14th century
H. (surviving) 16 cm, D. (foot, as restored) 8.4 cm
Blown; applied
Collection of Karl Amendt, Krefeld (LP 2010-20)

GOBLETS with a hollow stem and a broad foot have been found in archeological contexts of the 14th and 15th centuries. In many cases, the bowl is decorated with vertical ribs, and sometimes it has decoration that was blown in a dip mold.

Bibliography
Amendt Collection 2005, p. 81, no. 20.

46. BEAKER DECORATED WITH PRUNTS

Germany or an adjoining region to the south or east, 13th to 14th century
H. (surviving) 11.7 cm, D. (at highest point) 7.4 cm
Blown; applied
The Metropolitan Museum of Art, New York (06.141, gift of the Estate Abrau
   of the Russian Imperial Apanages, through Arthur R. Schultz)

THE BEAKER was found in a burial mound on the Abrau estate near Novorossiysk on the Black Sea coast of Russia. Other finds from burial mounds on the same estate include **47**, **48**, and perhaps **49**, and all four objects are assumed to be European. A beaker with the same proportions and similar prunts was found at Olginskoye, near Tuapse, which is southeast of Novorossiysk (Kramarovsky 1998, p. 100 and fig. 22.2). Perhaps the largest group of 13th-century and later glass vessels from this part of Russia was excavated in a cemetery at Belore-chensk, near Maykop. Seven burial mounds, of which three are Islamic and four are European, contained glass (*ibid.*, p. 97).

47. BEAKER DECORATED WITH PRUNTS

Germany or an adjoining region to the south or east,
*   13th to 14th century*
H. 9.7 cm, D. (rim) 8.3 cm
The Metropolitan Museum of Art, New York (06.143, gift of the Estate Abrau
*   of the Russian Imperial Apanages, through Arthur R. Schultz)*

LIKE ANOTHER prunted beaker (**46**), this object was discovered in a burial mound on the Abrau estate near Novorossiysk on the Black Sea coast of Russia. **46**, **47**, and **48** are indistinguishable visually from beakers made in Europe, and we conclude that they were imported through one of the Italian trading settlements in the Crimea. **49**, on the other hand, is of different glass and has a sheared rim that is not found on European glasses of the 13th and 14th centuries; it was probably made at a different time and/or place.

48. BEAKER WITH APPLIED DECORATION

Probably Germany, late 13th to early 14th century
H. 13.3 cm, D. (rim) 11.5 cm
Blown; applied
The Metropolitan Museum of Art, New York (06.140, gift of the Estate Abrau
of the Russian Imperial Apanages, through Arthur R. Schultz)

THE BEAKER was found in a burial mound on the Abrau estate near Novorossiysk on the Black Sea coast of Russia. It is, however, almost identical to beakers that, to judge from the find-places, were made in Germany and perhaps adjacent regions. Other finds from burial mounds on the same estate include prunted beakers (e.g., **46**, **47**, and perhaps **49**), and these, too, are very similar to beakers found in Europe.

49. BEAKER DECORATED WITH PRUNTS

Place and date of manufacture uncertain
H. (surviving) 11.4 cm, D. (at highest point) 9.5 cm
Blown; applied
The Metropolitan Museum of Art, New York (06.142, gift of the Estate Abrau
  of the Russian Imperial Apanages, through Arthur R. Schultz)

THIS BEAKER, like **46–48**, which are believed to be European, is said to have been found in a burial mound on the Abrau estate near Novorossiysk on the Black Sea coast of Russia. The small size of the prunts and the arrangement of some of them in groups of three are unusual, but they are matched on two smaller beakers found during excavations at Tarquinia in central Italy (Newby 1999, v. 2, p. 10, nos. 57 and 58 and fig. 8; Newby 2000, p. 259, fig. 1a and b).

The glass, however, is yellowish and very bubbly (unlike the glass of **46–48**), and it has a different chemical composition. These features, in addition to the beaker's almost pristine condition, raise the possibility that it is a modern imitation of a medieval vessel. A second possibility is that the beaker is medieval but was made in a different place, perhaps in a Crimean workshop that produced European-style glassware.

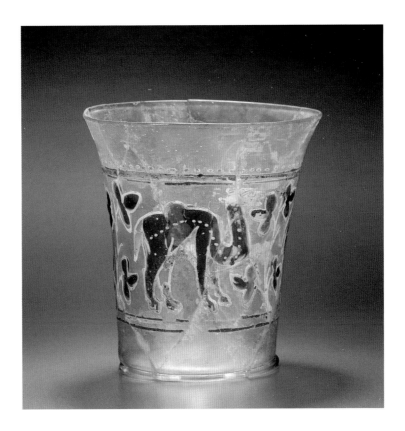

50. BEAKER WITH CAMELS

Probably Italy, Murano, late 13th to early 14th century
H. 8 cm, D. (rim) 7.7 cm
Blown; enameled
Collection of Karl Amendt, Krefeld (LP 2010-1)

THE DECORATION of this beaker, which was probably found in the Middle Rhine region of Germany, consists of two camels separated by sprays of leaves or flowers. Although we associate camels with North Africa and Asia, they were not unknown in medieval Europe. A camel appears in a street scene in Ambrogio Lorenzetti's fresco *The Effects of Good Government* (painted in 1338–1340), in the Palazzo Pubblico, Siena, and others are shown on stone reliefs in the Ca' Mastelli (14th century) and the Ca' Zen (16th century) in Venice (Howard 2000, pp. 150–151, figs. 181 and 183).

Bibliography
Amendt Collection 1987, pp. 34–35, no. 1; *Phönix aus Sand und Asche* 1988, pp. 142–143, no. 92.

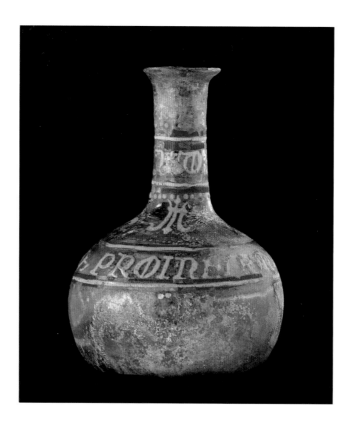

51. BOTTLE

Probably Italy, Venice, late 13th to early 14th century
H. 7.8 cm, D. (max.) 5.6 cm
Blown; enameled
Grand Curtius, Glass Department, Liège (B/1612)

THE BOTTLE is decorated with two inscriptions separated, on the shoulder, by four fleurs-de-lis. The inscriptions have suffered minor damage, and, in the past, reading them presented a challenge; indeed, they have been variously identified as Greek and as a mixture of Greek and Latin (Philippe 1970, p. 147; Philippe 1975, p. 9). In fact, they are Latin. The short inscription on the neck is "AMEN.D." (for "Amen, Domine," Amen, Lord). The second, longer inscription is "[ ]PROINFIRMIS" (for "Oleum pro infirmis," oil for the sick).

These inscriptions indicate that the bottle was intended to contain oil that had been blessed by a bishop for use in the sacrament of anointing the sick. In the Roman Catholic Church, anointing the sick was one of the seven sacraments of the New Testament.

The bottle was acquired in Rome, Italy, in 1922. Its earlier history is unknown.

Bibliography
Philippe 1975, pp. 8–11 (with earlier references);
Krueger 2002, p. 117.

52. *STANGENGLAS*

Bohemia, first half of the 15th century
H. (surviving, with metal foot) 37.5 cm, D. (max.) 6.8 cm
Blown; applied
Collection of Karl Amendt, Krefeld (LP 2010-137)

TALL, NARROW FLUTES decorated with dozens of very small prunts were made in Bohemia between the late 14th and mid-15th centuries. More than half of the fragmentary glass vessels of this period found in archeological excavations in Plzeň and Prague in the present-day Czech Republic are of this type, which is common at other sites in Bohemia but rare elsewhere. This example, however, was probably found in Mainz, Germany. The metal foot is a late medieval repair.

Bibliography
Amendt Collection 1987, pp. 91–92, no. 107; Amendt Collection 2005, p. 180, no. 137.

53. *KEULENGLAS*

Germany, 15th century
H. (as restored) 32.5 cm, D. (foot) 13.3 cm
Blown (in dip mold)
Collection of Karl Amendt, Krefeld (LP 2010-138)

KEULENGLÄSER (club-shaped beakers) are so called because the shape, with its bulging upper section, resembles that of a club (German, *Keule*). They were made in a large area of central and western Europe, extending from Bohemia to the Low Countries. This example may have been made in Bohemia and exported to Germany, unlike **54**, which resembles beakers produced in the southern Netherlands and northern France. The fluted surface was made by inserting the bubble of molten glass into a dip mold with 27 ribs, then twirling it on the blowpipe. About seven centimeters of the lower wall is missing and has been restored.

The object is believed to have been found in Mainz, Germany.

Bibliography
Amendt Collection 1987, p. 92, no. 108; *Amendt Collection* 2005, pp. 181 and 279–280, no. 138.

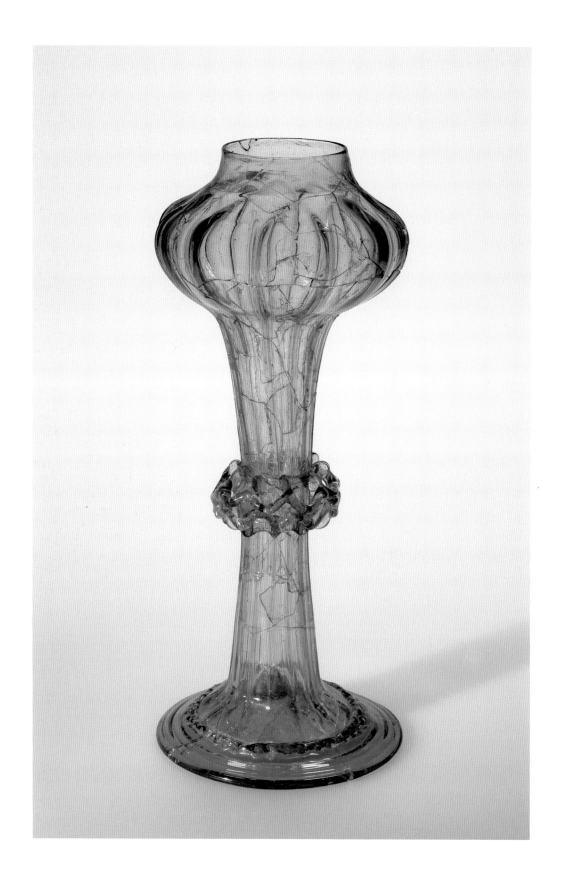

54. KEULENGLAS

Southern Netherlands or northern France, about 1500
H. 25.6 cm
Mold-blown; applied
The Corning Museum of Glass (2000.3.23)

THIS IS a fine example of the type of drinking vessel known in German as a *Keulenglas* and in Dutch as a *knotsbeker* (club glass or club beaker). The names refer to the vessel's distinctive shape, with a bowl that is tall and narrow except for a bulge under the rim. Club-shaped beakers were made in forest glasshouses in Bohemia, Germany, and the Low Countries, and in adjacent regions, between the late 14th and early 16th centuries. The largest *Keulengläser*, which are up to 50 centimeters tall, were intended for the consumption of beer, while smaller specimens were for drinking wine. Beakers shaped like **54** have been found in the southern Netherlands and northern France.

Bibliography
Guide to the Collections 2001, p. 64.

55. *STANGENGLAS* WITH CLAWS AND ANIMALS' HEADS

Germany, first half of the 16th century
H. 23.2 cm, D. (rim) 5.8 cm
Blown (in dip mold); applied
Collection of Karl Amendt, Krefeld (LP 2010-42)

A *STANGENGLAS* (the German word means "pole glass") is a tall, narrow cylindrical drinking vessel (hence the name "pole glass"), usually with a pedestal foot. Between the late 15th and mid-16th centuries, glassmakers in Germany produced large *Stangengläser* with elaborate applied decoration. The glass is colorless

or very pale green; the decoration is either the same color or a strongly contrasting color such as deep blue. The ornament sometimes consists of hollow "trunks" or "claws" similar to the decoration found on late Roman and early medieval beakers (such as **14**).

At least two other *Stangengläser* decorated with a band of claws surmounted by animals' heads are known, both with the same color scheme as **55**: (1) a fragment in the Museum Boijmans Van Beuningen, Rotterdam, the Netherlands (inv. no. 1096: *Phönix aus Sand und Asche* 1988, p. 402, no. 503), and (2) in the Museum Kunst Palast, Düsseldorf, Germany (inv. no. P 1964-22 A: *ibid.*, p. 403, no. 504). In both cases, the find-place is unknown.

This object was probably found in Cologne, Germany.

Bibliography
Amendt Collection 2005, p. 184, no. 142.

56. *STANGENGLAS* WITH ANIMALS' HEADS

Germany, late 15th to early 16th century
H. 22.8 cm, D. (rim) 4.9 cm
Blown (in dip mold); applied
Landesmuseum Württemberg, Stuttgart (1984-27)

THIS HANDSOME GLASS is made of transparent pale yellowish green glass, which is much lighter than forest glass, with deep blue applied ornament. The spiral decoration on the body was made by inflating the bubble of molten glass in a ribbed dip mold before the bubble was blown and tooled to make the intended shape. The animals' heads, which are found on other vessels of this date, were made in the manner described on page 169.

This *Stangenglas* was found, together with other objects, in the Cologne suburb of Eigelstein. The associated finds included a Siegburg stoneware beaker made about 1500. A second *Stangenglas* is said to have come from the same find-place. It is entirely possible that the second glass is **57** and that **56** and **57** are a pair.

Bibliography
Phönix aus Sand und Asche 1988, p. 400, no. 500.

57. *STANGENGLAS* DECORATED WITH ANIMALS' HEADS

Germany, late 15th to early 16th century
H. 22.5 cm, D. (foot) 9.6 cm
Blown (in dip mold); applied
Collection of Karl Amendt, Krefeld
   (LP 2010-141)

See **56**.

Bibliography
Amendt Collection 1987, pp. 94–95, no. 111; Phönix aus Sand und Asche 1988, p. 400, no. 501; Amendt Collection 2005, p. 182, no. 141.

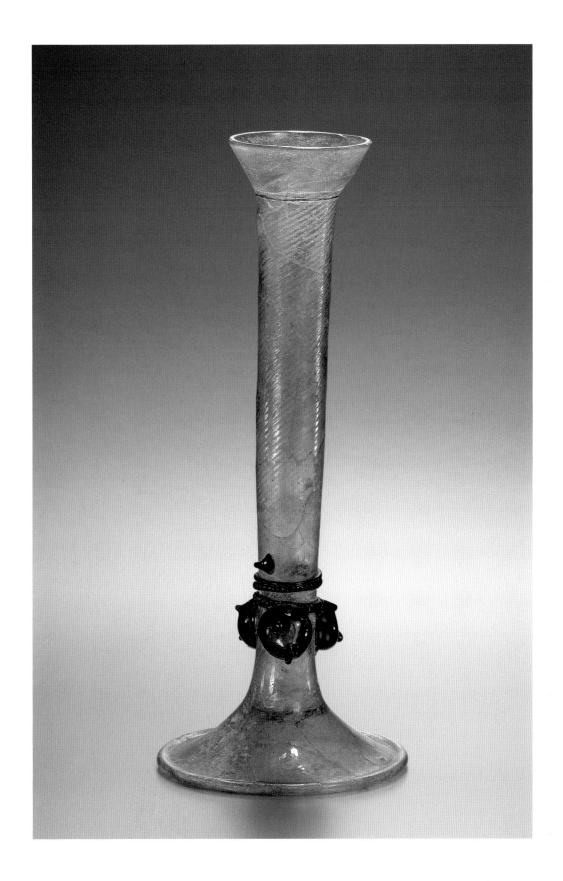

58. *STANGENGLAS* WITH APPLIED DECORATION

Germany, first half of the 16th century
H. 23.1 cm, D. (foot) 8 cm
Blown (in dip mold); applied
Glasmuseum Hentrich, Museum Kunst Palast, Düsseldorf (P 1978-44)

THE BODY of this glass has three different kinds of applied ornament: at the top and the bottom, two relatively thick horizontal trails that were drawn, one down and the other up, to form a continuous row of vertical stripes; above and below them, continuous horizontal trails that were flattened and notched with a roulette; and between the notched trails, an openwork "cage."

Other 16th-century vessels with trailed cages include a conical beaker in the LVR-Landesmuseum Bonn (91.0247: "Recent Important Acquisitions," *JGS*, v. 34, 1992, p. 128, no. 7) and a beaker in The Corning Museum of Glass (91.3.23).

Bibliography
Phönix aus Sand und Asche 1988, pp. 404–406, no. 508.

59. *STANGENGLAS* WITH APPLIED DECORATION

Germany, first half of the 16th century
H. 26.3 cm, D. (foot) 10.9 cm
Blown; applied
Collection of Karl Amendt, Krefeld (LP 2010-143)

THIS IS an unusually elaborate example of a *Stangenglas*. The rim and the upper wall were given a polygonal shape by inserting a tool with vertical "fins" into the semimolten glass. Two horizontal rows of hollow projections were made by applying blobs of hot glass to the wall of the vessel. The hot glass melted the wall at the point of contact, and the maker created a protrusion by blowing into the partly formed vessel. The lower row of four schematic heads of animals was created first, followed by the upper row of "claws" or "trunks." The other ornament was made by applying and manipulating trails of molten glass.

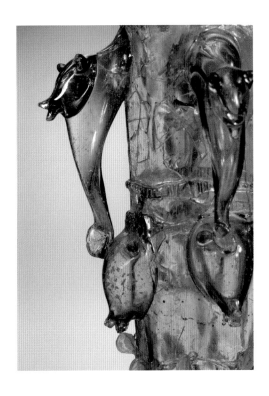

Bibliography
Amendt Collection 1987, pp. 95–96, no. 112; *Phönix aus Sand und Asche* 1988, p. 404, no. 507; *Amendt Collection* 2005, p. 186, no. 143.

60. BEAKER WITH ANIMALS' HEADS

Germany, first half of the 16th century
H. 10.7 cm, D. (rim) 7.3 cm
Blown; applied
Collection of Karl Amendt, Krefeld (LP 2010-124)

THIS IS a remarkable object. It is one of only a very small number of beakers decorated with animals' heads in relief. (For a forest glass beaker with a row of six animals' heads, see *Amendt Collection* 2005, p. 170, no. 123.) The intense blue color of the beaker is also unusual. (Another deep blue object, with a short stem and a hollow triangular foot, is shown in *ibid.*, p. 172, no. 125.)

This beaker was presumably found in Mainz, Germany.

Bibliography
Amendt Collection 2005, p. 171, no. 124.

61. BEAKER WITH CLAWS AND ANIMALS' HEADS

Germany, second half of the 16th century
H. (surviving) 6.4 cm, W. (across animals' heads) 5.5 cm
Blown; applied
Collection of Karl Amendt, Krefeld (LP 2010-144)

THIS ALMOST grotesquely elaborate beaker was made with the same techniques and satisfied the same tastes as *Stangengläser* such as **55–57** and **59**, and as other beakers such as **60**. In every case, the decoration consists of hollow "claws" and/or hollow animals' heads. Here, the claws and heads are accompanied by a row of prunts below the rim (which is missing) and a horizontal trail with vertical ribs and notches made with a wheel-like tool.

The object is said to have been found in Liège, Belgium.

Bibliography
Amendt Collection 1987, p. 87, no. 98; *Amendt Collection* 2005, p. 188, no. 144.

62. INKWELL(?)

Place of manufacture unknown, probably 16th century
H. 13.6 cm, D. (base) 18.6 cm
Blown (two gathers); applied
Collection of Karl Amendt, Krefeld (LP 2010-163)

THE OBJECT has an open, globular reservoir resting on a broad foot shaped like the mouth of a trumpet. The diameter of the foot makes the object very stable, and the small opening and limited capacity of the reservoir suggest that it was intended to be an inkwell.

Erwin Baumgartner (in *Amendt Collection* 1987 and 2005: see below) draws attention to a similar object, clearly an inkwell, in the portrait of Cardinal Albrecht of Brandenburg as Saint Jerome, painted by Lucas Cranach the Elder (1472–1553) in 1527, now in the Gemäldegalerie of the Staatliche Museen zu Berlin.

The object is believed to have been found in Alkmaar, the Netherlands.

Bibliography
Amendt Collection 1987, p. 106, no. 129; *Amendt Collection* 2005, pp. 204 and 286–287, no. 163.

63. BEAKER

Germany or the southern Netherlands, 14th century
H. 6.8 cm, D. (rim) 7.1 cm
Blown (in dip mold)
LVR-Landesmuseum Bonn (57.4)

THIS BEAKER was discovered in 1955 beneath the high altar in the parish church at Kendenich, near Cologne, Germany. The beaker, together with other relics, was found in a lead casket. A similar beaker is in the Diözesanmuseum in Trier, Germany (Rademacher 1933, p. 98 and pl. 29b). Another parallel, probably from Cologne, has a blue trail around the rim (*Phönix aus Sand und Asche* 1988, p. 300, no. 343).

Bibliography
Phönix aus Sand und Asche 1988, p. 300, no. 344.

64. BEAKER

Germany, 15th century
H. 7.4 cm, D. (rim) 7.7 cm
Blown (in dip mold)
Museum für Angewandte Kunst Frankfurt, Frankfurt am Main (13414)
Formerly in the Pfoh Collection

64–70 are forest glass beakers with mold-blown decoration. All of them were blown in dip molds with ribbed or diamond-shaped decoration. The spiraling decoration of **64** was produced by blowing the bubble of molten glass into a mold with vertical ribs, withdrawing the bubble from the mold, and twisting the glass on the blowpipe to create a pattern of spiral ribs.

Bibliography
Phönix aus Sand und Asche 1988, p. 308, no. 360.

65. BEAKER

Germany, 15th century
H. 6.5 cm, D. (rim) 7.1 cm
Blown (in dip mold)
LVR-Landesmuseum Bonn (68.0422)
Formerly in the Bremen Collection

UNLIKE **64**, which was inflated in a dip mold and twisted in one direction to produce a pattern of spirals, this beaker was inserted into the mold twice. After the bubble of molten glass had been inflated in the mold and twisted to create spiral ribs, it was reinserted, withdrawn, and twisted in the opposite direction to produce a crisscross effect.

Bibliography
Phönix aus Sand und Asche 1988, p. 308, no. 359.

66. BEAKER

Germany, early 16th century
H. 7.5 cm, D. (rim) 7.7 cm
Blown (in dip mold)
LVR-Landesmuseum Bonn (68.0428)
Formerly in the Bremen Collection

66, LIKE **65**, was decorated by inserting the bubble of molten glass into a ribbed dip mold not once but twice. A beaker with similar ornament, in the Diözesanmuseum Rottenburg, was discovered in the high altar of the church at Reichenbach, which was consecrated in 1519.

This object was probably found at Bopfingen, Baden-Württemberg, in southwestern Germany.

Bibliography
Phönix aus Sand und Asche 1988, p. 375, no. 462.

67. BEAKER

Germany, late 15th century
H. 9 cm, D. (rim) 7.8 cm
Blown (in dip mold)
The Corning Museum of Glass (69.3.6)

65–67 have crisscross decoration made by inserting the molten glass on the blowpipe into a ribbed dip mold on two occasions. On the first occasion, the glass was withdrawn from the mold and twisted in one direction; the second time, it was withdrawn and twisted in the opposite direction. The beaker was shaped by manipulating the glass after it had been decorated in a straight-sided mold.

For two similar beakers, see *Amendt Collection* 2005, p. 129, nos. 81 and especially 82, both of which are said to have been found in Cologne, Germany.

This object is said to have been found in or near Cologne, Germany.

Bibliography
Masterpieces of Germanic Glass 1979, p. 20, no. 1.

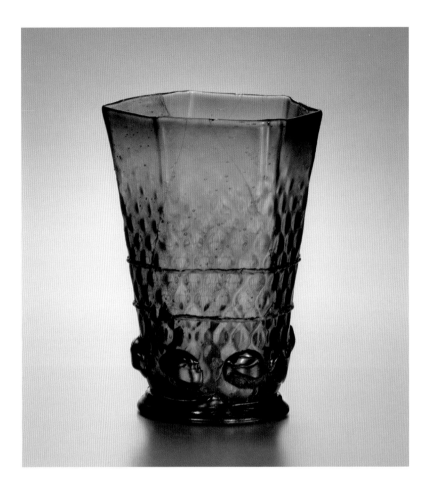

68. BEAKER WITH SIX SIDES

Germany, first half of the 16th century
H. 10.7 cm, D. (foot) 5.4 cm
Blown (in dip mold); applied
Collection of Karl Amendt, Krefeld (LP 2010-95)

THE BEAKER was formed and decorated in three stages. First, the bubble of molten glass was inflated in a dip mold with an overall pattern of lozenges. Next, glass was applied in three operations: (1) two narrow trails were attached to the lower wall to make continuous horizontal ribs, (2) a row of prunts was applied to the bottom of the wall, and (3) another trail was wound several times around the junction of the wall and the base to form a coiled foot-ring. Finally, the mouth of the beaker was given its hexagonal shape by inserting a tool with six vertical "fins."

Bibliography
Amendt Collection 1987, pp. 77–78, no. 78; *Phönix aus Sand und Asche* 1988, p. 360, no. 441; *Amendt Collection* 2005, p. 140, no. 95.

69. BEAKER WITH EIGHT SIDES

Germany, 15th century
H. 7 cm, W. (rim) 7.9 cm
Blown (in dip mold); tooled
Glasmuseum Hentrich, Museum Kunst Palast,
  Düsseldorf (1936-10)

SMALL BEAKERS decorated with vertical or spiraling ribs made by inflating the bubble of molten glass in a dip mold were common drinking vessels in Italy, Germany, and other parts of Europe in and after the 14th century. This example is unusual in that the rim and upper wall are octagonal. A modern glassworker would create the octagonal form by inserting a tool with eight vertical "fins," which shapes the semimolten glass.

Bibliography
Phönix aus Sand und Asche 1988, pp. 309–310, no. 362.

70. BEAKER WITH FOOT

Probably Germany, early 16th century
H. 10.7 cm, D. (foot) 7.2 cm
Blown (in dip mold); applied
The Corning Museum of Glass (90.3.15)

EXCEPT FOR its diminutive height, this narrow beaker resembles a *Stangenglas*. The decoration, which was formed in a dip mold, consists of 10 vertical rows of shallow protrusions.

71. *MAIGELEIN*

Germany or the Low Countries, about 1500
H. 3.5 cm, D. (rim) 7.8 cm
Blown (in dip mold)
The Corning Museum of Glass (69.3.14)

THIS SHALLOW CUP belongs to a large group of mold-blown vessels made in Germany and the Low Countries from the beginning of the 16th century. The forms include beakers such as **66** and *Maigeleien*, and the ornament consists either of ribs or of crossed ribs made by inserting the bubble of hot glass into the dip mold twice.

Bibliography
Masterpieces of Germanic Glass 1979, p. 20, no. 2.

72. BEAKER WITH APPLIED DECORATION

Germany, about 1500–1550
H. 7.1 cm, D. (rim) 4.7 cm
Blown; applied
Diözesanmuseum Freising (P 851-22)

THE COLOR of this beaker is unusual. The wall and the prunts are of transparent light bluish glass, while the trail spirally wound around the rim and the horizontal trail above the row of prunts are deep blue.

The beaker was found in the diocese of Freising, Germany, but the exact find-place is not recorded.

Bibliography
Phönix aus Sand und Asche 1988, pp. 360–361, no. 442.

73. BEAKER WITH APPLIED DECORATION

Germany, beginning of the 16th century
H. 7.4 cm, D. (rim) 5.4 cm
Blown; applied
Museum für Kunst und Gewerbe, Hamburg (1913.268)
Formerly in the Schnütgen and Lanna Collections

THE SHAPE of this small beaker is identical to that of numerous *Krautstrünke* (such as **74–81**), which were popular in Germany and adjoining regions in the late 15th and early 16th centuries. Here, however, instead of applied blobs, the ornament consists of four horizontal trails, three of which have been manipulated to form series of upward-pointing projections.

Bibliography
Phönix aus Sand und Asche 1988, p. 331, no. 396.

74. *KRAUTSTRUNK*

Germany, first half of the 16th century
H. 6.3 cm, D. (rim) 3.1 cm
Blown; applied
Collection of Karl Amendt, Krefeld (LP 2010-48)

THE GERMAN TERM *Krautstrunk* (cabbage stalk) refers to beakers with large prunts that have been pinched to form a central point or nipple.

Numerous *Krautstrünke* of the early 16th century have a wide cup-shaped mouth, a narrow egg-shaped body, and an applied foot worked into small, bulbous "toes." The walls of these beakers are decorated with two or three horizontal rows of wide, shallow prunts with diminutive nipples.

The beaker is said to have been found in Cologne, Germany.

Bibliography
Amendt Collection 1987, p. 60, no. 40; *Phönix aus Sand und Asche* 1988, pp. 341–342, no. 411; *Amendt Collection* 2005, p. 104, no. 48.

75. *KRAUTSTRUNK*

Germany, late 15th to early 16th century
H. 11.7 cm, D. (rim) 8.3 cm
Blown; applied
The Corning Museum of Glass (54.3.245)

SMALL, PRUNTED *Krautstrünke* were widely used in Germany and adjoining regions in the late 15th and early 16th centuries. They were also employed as containers for relics: bones or other objects associated with saints, which were venerated by pilgrims and other believers.

Among the many *Krautstrünke* similar to this example are beakers in the Diözesanmuseum Rottenburg in Germany that were sealed in or before 1498, and a beaker from the Church of St. Vincent in Pleif, Switzerland, that dates from the beginning of the 16th century (*Phönix aus Sand und Asche* 1988, pp. 339–340, nos. 405–407).

76. *KRAUTSTRUNK*

Germany, beginning of the 16th century
H. 10 cm, D. (rim) 8.1 cm
Blown; applied
LVR-Landesmuseum Bonn (68.0486)
Formerly in the Bremen Collection

SIXTEENTH-CENTURY *Krautstrünke* are sturdy drinking glasses, and they survive in relatively large quantities. The fairly large, pointed prunts represent a transitional form between the smaller pointed prunts and the larger, flat prunts that became popular in the late 15th and early 16th centuries (see **77–81**).

This beaker is believed to have been found in the church of Saint Martin at Leutkirch in the Allgäu region of southern Germany.

Bibliography
Phönix aus Sand und Asche 1988, p. 340, no. 408.

77. KRAUTSTRUNK

Germany or Switzerland, first quarter of the 16th century
H. 10.2 cm, D. (rim) 7.1 cm
Blown; applied
Museum zu Allerheiligen, Schaffhausen (16050)

THIS BEAKER is typical of small forest glass drinking vessels made in Germany in the early 16th century. The characteristics of these vessels include the cup-shaped rim, the roughly egg-shaped body, and a single row of large, flat prunts.

The object was found at Illgau in Schwyz canton, Switzerland.

Bibliography
Phönix aus Sand und Asche 1988, p. 345, no. 415.

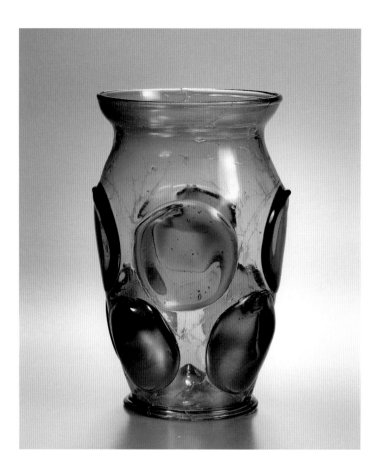

78. *KRAUTSTRUNK*

Germany, about 1510–1530
H. 17.6 cm, D. (rim) 10.8 cm
Blown; applied
Collection of Karl Amendt, Krefeld (LP 2010-40)

See **76**.

Two types of bases are found on these small *Krautstrünke*. In the first type, represented by **74–77**, **79**, and **81**, the trail at the junction of the wall and the base has been tooled into a series of "toes" (which are hardly apparent on **81**); in the second type, represented by **78** and **80**, the trail was not turned into a row of toes.

This beaker is believed to have been found in Mainz, Germany.

Bibliography
Amendt Collection 2005, p. 96, no. 40.

79. *KRAUTSTRUNK*

Germany, 15th century
H. 9.6 cm, D. (rim) 6 cm
Blown; applied
LVR-Landesmuseum Bonn (35.254)

THIS BEAKER resembles **78**, although the latter has a coiled rather than a "toed" base. Until 1935, **79** was in a private collection in Cologne, but we have no reason to suppose that it was necessarily found in that city.

Bibliography
Phönix aus Sand und Asche 1988, p. 298, no. 342.

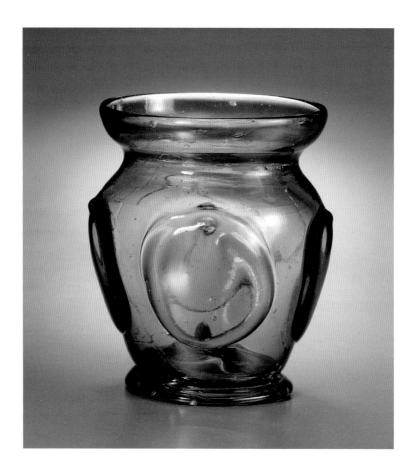

80. *KRAUTSTRUNK*

Germany, first quarter of the 16th century
H. 8.3 cm, D. (rim) 6.8 cm
Blown; applied
Collection of Karl Amendt, Krefeld (LP 2010-42)

THE COILED BASE of this forest glass beaker resembles the coiled base of other *Krautstrünke*, such as **78**.

The beaker is believed to have been found in Mainz, Germany.

Bibliography
Amendt Collection 2005, p. 99, no. 42.

81. *KRAUTSTRUNK*

Germany, 15th to early 16th century
H. 7.8 cm, D. (rim) 5.8 cm
Blown; applied
The Corning Museum of Glass (50.3.38)

THIS OBJECT, like **74–77**, and **79**, has a "toed" base, although the toes are less prominent than on the other objects. A somewhat similar example, with three horizontal rows of prunts, was found during excavations at Christ Church, Aschaffenburg, Germany (*Phönix aus Sand und Asche* 1988, p. 298, no. 341).

Bibliography
Masterpieces of Germanic Glass 1979, p. 20, no. 3.

82. *KRAUTSTRUNK*

Germany, about 1500
H. 5 cm, D. (rim) 9.5 cm
Blown; applied
Collection of Karl Amendt, Krefeld (LP 2010-44)

WHILE THE MAJORITY of small late 15th- and 16th-century *Krautstrünke* are beakers with a roughly egg-shaped body (such as **74–81**), others (such as **82** and **83**) are short and have a relatively wide body.

This example is said to have been found in Cologne, Germany. For a similar vessel, see Ritsema van Eck and Zijlstra-Zweens 1993, p. 117, no. 159.

Bibliography
Amendt Collection 1987, pp. 56–57, no. 35; *Phönix aus Sand und Asche* 1988, p. 348, no. 421; *Amendt Collection* 2005, p. 101, no. 44.

83. KRAUTSTRUNK

Germany, second quarter of the 16th century
H. 5.8 cm, D. (rim) 6.9 cm
Blown; applied
LVR-Landesmuseum Bonn (68.0487)
Formerly in the Bremen Collection

See **82.**
The vessel is said to have been found in the Allgäu region of southern Germany.

Bibliography
Phönix aus Sand und Asche 1988, p. 341, no. 410.

84. BERKEMEYER

Germany, second half of the 16th century
H. 9 cm, D. (rim) 8.9 cm
Blown; applied
Collection of Karl Amendt, Krefeld (LP 2010-110)

A *BERKEMEYER* is a beaker with a large funnel-shaped mouth. *Berkemeyer* were made in Germany in the 16th and 17th centuries. According to Ritsema van Eck and Zijlstra-Zweens (1993, p. 113), the term *berkemeier* is found in Dutch documents of the 16th century, but not in the Middle Dutch or Middle High German dialects, and this indicates that the origin of the name lies in the northern Netherlands. (The spelling used here is modern German.)

This *Berkemeyer* is said to have been found in Cologne, Germany. For a very similar example, but with a "toed" foot, see *ibid.*, p. 124, no. 171 (in the Rijksmuseum, Amsterdam, inv. no. RBK 14510).

Bibliography
Amendt Collection 1987, p. 81, no. 86; *Amendt Collection* 2005, p. 157, no. 110.

85. *BERKEMEYER*

Germany, mid-16th century
H. 7.9 cm, D. (rim) 7.3 cm
Blown (in dip mold); applied
Collection of Karl Amendt, Krefeld (LP 2010-109)

THIS *BERKEMEYER* combines mold-blown decoration with two rows of large, rather flat prunts and an applied trail at the edge of the base, which has been pinched into a series of "toes." A similar beaker was found in 1986 in Heidelberg, Germany, during excavations in the Kornmarkt. Associated finds indicated that the object had been buried in the first half of the 16th century (*Phönix aus Sand und Asche* 1988, pp. 364–365, no. 449).

This example was probably found in Cologne, Germany.

Bibliography
Amendt Collection 1987, p. 80, no. 85; *Phönix aus Sand und Asche* 1988, p. 366, no. 453.

86. STONEWARE *BERKEMEYER*

Germany, Siegburg, 16th century
H. 8.7 cm, D. (rim) 6.5–6.8 cm
Thrown; applied, tooled
LVR-Landesmuseum Bonn (49.1)

THIS IS a yellowish salt-glazed stoneware version of a glass *Berkemeyer*, made at Siegburg, 12 kilometers northeast of Bonn.

Siegburg was a major center for the production of salt-glazed stoneware between the late 14th and early 17th centuries. Around the middle of the 16th century, Cologne temporarily became the leading producer of German stoneware, but the industry continued at Siegburg until 1632, when the city was destroyed during the Thirty Years' War (1618–1648). Subsequently, Westerwald, where Siegburg potters had established manufacturing about 1590, became the most prolific center of stoneware production in Germany.

Bibliography
Phönix aus Sand und Asche 1988, p. 366, no. 452.

87. SCHEUER

Germany, late 15th to mid-16th century
H. 8 cm, D. (rim) 5.8 cm
Blown; applied
Collection of Karl Amendt, Krefeld (LP 2010-57)

See **42**.

Scheuern, often furnished with a cover in the form of an inverted cup or bowl—and for this reason known as *Doppelscheuern* ("double *Scheuern*")—were first made of wood in the 14th century. In the 15th century, they were imitated in silver, rock crystal, and glass. Glass *Scheuern* were made in Venice, presumably for the German market, as well as in Germany.

In a sermon published in 1562, Johann Mathesius, a priest in Jáchymov (Joachims-thal), northwestern Bohemia, described how, before a prince or a gentleman drank from a *Doppelscheuer*, his servant would drink from the cover to make sure that the beverage was not poisoned (Lanmon 1993, p. 78).

This object was probably found in Mainz, Germany.

Bibliography
Phönix aus Sand und Asche 1988, p. 382, no. 474;
Amendt Collection 2005, p. 113, no. 57.

88. *SCHEUER*

Germany, first quarter of the 16th century
H. 9 cm, D. (rim) 5.6 cm
Blown; applied
Collection of Karl Amendt, Krefeld (LP 2010-54)

THIS *SCHEUER* is made of deep green forest glass and is decorated with prunts arranged
in vertical rows. Alternate rows have two and
three prunts.

An unglazed brownish stoneware *Scheuer*
made at Siegburg, near Bonn, Germany, has a
similar form (*Phönix aus Sand und Asche* 1988,
p. 385, no. 482).

This glass *Scheuer* is said to have been found
in Speyer, Germany.

Bibliography
Amendt Collection 1987, p. 59, no. 38; *Phönix aus
Sand und Asche* 1988, pp. 383–384, no. 479; *Amendt
Collection* 2005, p. 110, no. 54.

89. BOWL

Germany, first half of the 16th century
H. 6.4 cm, D. (rim) 10.2 cm
Blown; applied
Collection of Karl Amendt, Krefeld (LP 2010-58)
Formerly in the Stieg and Baumgartner Collections

THIS very unusual bowl has a handle resembling the handles of *Scheuern* such as **42**, **87**, **88**, and **109**. The low conical foot was made by winding a trail of glass six times around and below the bottom of the wall. The deep blue of the glass is reminiscent of the color of applied decoration on some *Stangengläser* of the early to mid-16th century (e.g., **55–58**).

The object is said to have been found in the vicinity of Cologne, Germany.

Bibliography
Amendt Collection 2005, p. 114, no. 58.

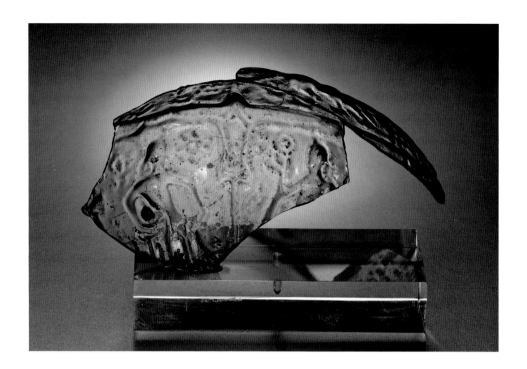

90.   FRAGMENTS OF A BOWL(?)

Germany, late 13th to early 14th century
H. (surviving) about 7.8 cm, D. (max.)
about 16 cm
Blown (in mold with two sections)
Collection of Karl Amendt, Krefeld
(LP 2010-223a [upper band]
and LP 2010-44 [lower band])

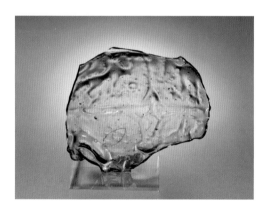

THE FRAGMENTS, which are decorated in low relief, appear to be parts of a bowl. The decoration consists of two horizontal bands containing human figures, creatures, and other elements. The surviving part of the upper band (right) includes two griffins facing each other on either side of a pillar, while the lower band (above) includes (on the left) a woman with her hands on her hips and (on the right) a man holding a ring in his raised right hand, again facing each other on either side of a pillar or column, which branches at the top.

Fragments of a beaker blown in a mold with two sections have been found in an archeological context containing material of the late 13th century and the first decade of the 14th century at Magdeburg, Germany (*Phönix aus Sand und Asche* 1988, p. 225, no. 213).

Bibliography
Amendt Collection 1987, pp. 45–47, no. 16; *Phönix aus Sand und Asche* 1988, pp. 225–226, no. 214; *Amendt Collection* 2005, pp. 84–85, no. 23.

91. RING BEAKER

Germany or Bohemia, 16th century
H. 10.8 cm, D. (rim) 7.6 cm
Blown; applied
The Corning Museum of Glass (79.3.732, gift of The Ruth Bryan Strauss
   Memorial Foundation)
Formerly in the collections of H. Schiffton, A. Vecht, and Jerome Strauss (S309)

THIS RING BEAKER (German, *Ring-* or *Ringelbecher*) has an unusual combination of features. First, the straight, tapering side widens toward the base, so that the bottom of the vessel is almost hemispherical. Second, there are three varieties of applied decoration. A narrow trail was wound around the wall eight times to form a spiral from just below the rim to just above the base, after which it was notched with a tool; three diminutive loops were attached to the upper wall, each of which supports a ring; and a second bubble of molten glass was applied to the base and drawn up the lower wall to make a wavelike pattern in low relief. This wavelike effect is very similar to the "lily pad" decoration produced at some American glass factories in the 19th century.

Bibliography
Strauss Collection 1955, p. 39, no. 91.

92. MINIATURE HORN

Germany, perhaps 15th century
H. 9.8 cm, D. (rim) 4.2 cm
Blown (in dip mold)
Glasmuseum Hentrich, Museum Kunst Palast,
   Düsseldorf (1936-33)

THE PATTERN in low relief was produced by inflating the bubble of molten glass in a dip mold with vertical ribs; the swirled effect was created during further inflation after the glass had been removed from the mold. Despite its diminutive size, the horn may have been used as a drinking glass, perhaps for hard liquor. It is also possible, as Rademacher (1933, p. 41) suggested, that it contained paint or ink. Rademacher noted another miniature glass horn, but without mold-blown ribs, in the Historisches Museum der Pfalz Speyer in Speyer, Germany (*ibid.*, pl. 4d).

Bibliography
Phönix aus Sand und Asche 1988, p. 438, no. 553
(with earlier references).

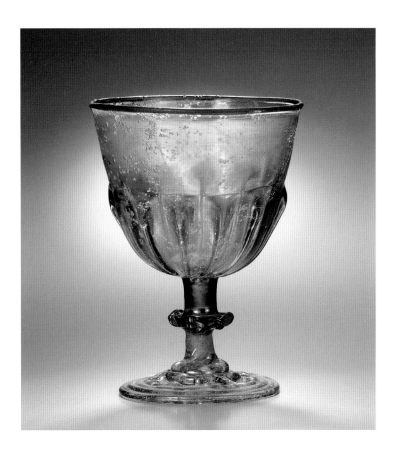

93. GOBLET

Germany, first half of the 16th century
H. 11.8 cm, D. (rim) 8.9 cm
Blown; applied
Collection of Karl Amendt, Krefeld (LP 2010-116)

GOBLETS with a ribbed bowl (including **93**) are attributed to the first half of the 16th century, as are beakers with a combination of vertical ribs and a deep blue trail on the rim (for example, *Amendt Collection* 2005, p. 164, no. 117, and p. 167, no. 120).

This goblet may have been found in Cologne, Germany.

Bibliography
Amendt Collection 1987, pp. 84–85, no. 93; *Phönix aus Sand und Asche* 1988, p. 416, no. 522.

94. *STANGENGLAS*

Switzerland or southwestern Germany, 16th century
H. 24.7 cm, D. (rim) 11.4 cm
Blown; applied
The Corning Museum of Glass (92.3.4)

FOREST GLASS *Stangengläser* decorated with vertical rows of prunts were popular in Germany and adjoining regions in the late 15th and early 16th centuries. Rademacher (1933, p. 150 and pl. 55a) published a close parallel from Mainz, Germany, and a similar vessel is in the Historisches Museum Basel in Switzerland (*Phönix aus Sand und Asche* 1988, p. 395, no. 493).

95. STANGENGLAS

Germany, 15th to 16th century
H. 21.5 cm, D. (rim) 7.7 cm
Blown; applied
The Corning Museum of Glass (90.3.13)

See **94**.

This example was found in Mainz, Germany.

96. STANGENGLAS

Germany, 16th century
H. 19.5 cm, D. (rim) 7.7 cm
Blown; applied
Museum für Kunst und Gewerbe, Hamburg (1919.216)

See **94** and **95**. This example has six vertical rows of ornament, each with seven or eight prunts with prominent, pointed nipples.

Bibliography
Phönix aus Sand und Asche 1988, p. 394, no. 491.

97.   BICONICAL BOTTLE

Germany, late 15th to early 16th century
H. 19.4 cm, D. (max.) 9.8 cm
Blown
LVR-Landesmuseum Bonn (68.0539)
Formerly in the Bremen Collection

BOTTLES of this distinctive form were popular in Germany for at least 200 years. One example is illustrated in a manuscript created in 1425 (see page 45), while another was found on the site of the Ziroff glass factory in Spessart, Germany, which operated for a short time between 1627 and 1631 (see bibliography).

This bottle was probably found in Würzburg, Germany, in 1962.

Bibliography
Phönix aus Sand und Asche 1988, p. 420, no. 527.

98. BICONICAL BOTTLE

Germany, 15th century
H. 16.4 cm, D. (max.) 12.3 cm
Blown
Collection of Karl Amendt, Krefeld (LP 2010-59)

A BOTTLE of this type is clearly illustrated in a manuscript of the "De universo" of Rabanus Maurus, written in Germany or the Tyrol in 1425. The manuscript is in the Biblioteca Apostolica Vaticana (*Codice Palatino Latino* 291, fol. 211v).

This example is said to have been found in the region of Speyer and Worms, Germany.

Bibliography
Amendt Collection 1987, p. 64, no. 46; Amendt Collection 2005, p. 115, no. 59.

99. BICONICAL BOTTLE

Germany, 15th century
H. 10.4 cm, D. (max.) 8 cm
Blown
The Corning Museum of Glass (91.3.41)

See **97** and **98**.
The bottle was found in Mainz, Germany.

100. BOTTLE

Germany, late 13th to early 14th century
H. 15.6 cm, D. (max.) 8.8 cm
Blown
The Corning Museum of Glass (91.3.24)

THE MOST distinctive feature of this bottle is the presence, near the widest part of the body, of a continuous tubular rib on the inside of the wall. Bottles with internal ribs have been found in several parts of Europe, both north and south of the Alps, in contexts that range from the 12th to 14th centuries.

Parallels for this example, which is said to have been found in Mainz, Germany, have been excavated in Basel, Switzerland, and in Höxter and Nuremberg, Germany (*Phönix aus Sand und Asche* 1988, pp. 267–268, nos. 296–299).

101. *KUTTROLF* OR *ANGSTER* WITH TWO TUBES

Germany, 15th century
H. 20.5 cm, D. (max.) 10.1 cm
Blown; tooled
Collection of Karl Amendt, Krefeld (LP 2010-62)

THE GERMAN WORD *Kuttrolf* is commonly used to refer to a flask with the neck divided into two or more tubes.

The first such vessels were made in central Europe in the Roman period. They were produced from time to time in the early Middle Ages, before becoming popular in the 14th century.

Although the shape appears to be relatively sophisticated, medieval *Kuttrolfe* or *Angster* were never made of decolorized or strongly colored glass, and if they have mounts, these are almost always of pewter or some other base metal.

This example may have been found in Mainz, Germany.

Bibliography
Amendt Collection 1987, p. 65, no. 49; *Phönix aus Sand und Asche* 1988, p. 323, no. 385; *Amendt Collection* 2005, p. 118, no. 62.

102. *KUTTROLF* OR *ANGSTER* WITH FIVE TUBES

Probably Germany, 14th to 15th century
H. 20.5 cm, D. (max.) 7.1 cm
Blown
The Corning Museum of Glass (56.3.22)

KUTTROLFE usually have a funnel-shaped rim. It seems likely, therefore, that the rim of this example was broken and the vessel was repaired by attaching a base metal top with a stopper.

The object is thought to have been found in the Netherlands.

Bibliography
Phönix aus Sand und Asche 1988, pp. 320–321, no. 382.

103. *KUTTROLF* OR *ANGSTER* WITH FIVE TUBES

Germany, 14th to 15th century
H. 18.8 cm, D. (max.) 8.6 cm
Blown
Glasmuseum Hentrich, Museum Kunst Palast, Düsseldorf (P 1940-43)

THE NECK of this example has been squeezed to create five narrow tubes. *Kuttrolf* is onomatopoeic (that is, the word imitates the sound made by the object it denotes). In this case, the word is thought to imitate the gurgling of liquid passing through the tubes. It is possible, however, that flasks with divided necks had a different name: *Angster* (from the Latin adjective *angustus*, "narrow"), which referred to the narrowness of the tubes. Both names were used to describe glass flasks in German documents of the 14th and 15th centuries.

Bibliography
Phönix aus Sand und Asche 1988, p. 320, no. 381.

104. LAMP

Germany, 15th century
H. 13.5 cm, D. (rim) 11.4 cm
Blown
Collection of Karl Amendt, Krefeld (LP 2010-157)

LAMPS with a bowl- or beaker-shaped upper portion and a narrow stem were placed, usually in groups, in metal hangers suspended by chains from the ceiling or a horizontal beam or bracket. They have a long history, which extends back at least to the fifth century A.D. In late antiquity, they were common in the eastern Mediterranean but unusual in the west, although they have been found, for example, at Rome and Carthage (Whitehouse 1997, pp. 194–195, no. 340).

Lamps of this type were commonly used in medieval Europe and the Islamic world. Their distribution in later medieval Europe was very wide, embracing Lübeck, Germany, in the north (*Phönix aus Sand und Asche* 1988, p. 437, no. 551); England in the west (Tyson 2000, pp. 141–147); and Prague, Bohemia, in the east (*Phönix aus Sand und Asche* 1988, p. 437, no. 550). Numerous examples are illustrated in paintings of this period: for example, in frescoes by Giotto di Bondone in the Scrovegni Chapel, Padua, executed in 1303–1305 (see page 54, Figure 19).

104 is said to have been found in Mainz, Germany.

Bibliography
Amendt Collection 1987, p. 103, no. 125; *Amendt Collection* 2005, p. 198, no. 157.

105.   DISH WITH OPENWORK FOOT

Possibly Germany, 15th or early 16th century
H. 5.5 cm, D. (rim) 7.8 cm
Blown; applied
Collection of Karl Amendt, Krefeld (LP 2010-22)

ALMOST EVERY FEATURE of this object is unusual. The opaque red glass has parallels among other late medieval (and later) objects, but these are rare; two 16th-century *Scheuern* appear in *Phönix aus Sand und Asche* 1988, pp. 382–383, nos. 475 (**109** in this catalog) and 476. The trailed openwork foot with six pinched "toes" appears to be unique, although some 15th- and 16th-century German goblets and beakers rest on circular foot-rings separated from the bases by openwork. The existence of such openwork feet forms the basis for attributing the dish to the 15th century or thereabouts.

The object was probably found in Aachen, Germany.

Bibliography
Amendt Collection 1987, pp. 44–45, no. 15; *Phönix aus Sand und Asche* 1988, p. 416, no. 523; *Amendt Collection* 2005, pp. 83 and 251–252, no. 22.

106. BEAKER WITH PRUNTED DECORATION AND OPENWORK FOOT

Germany, about 1500–1550
H. 9.9 cm, D. (rim) 7 cm
Blown; applied
The Corning Museum of Glass (79.3.178, bequest of Jerome Strauss)
Formerly in the Seligman and Strauss (S612) Collections

THIS OBJECT is perhaps the only intact example of a small group of prunted beakers with conical bowls and openwork feet formed by trailing. A very similar but fragmentary beaker was found during excavations in Maastricht, southeastern Netherlands, in association with pottery datable to the end of the 15th century or the beginning of the 16th century. Other beakers of this type appear in paintings by two Netherlandish artists of the first quarter of the 16th century: the Master of the Mansi Magdalen (active 1510–1525) and the Master of 1518 (*The Last Supper* in the Musées Royaux des Beaux-Arts de Belgique, Brussels). Openwork trailed feet are also found on *Scheuern* (such as **109**) and goblets (such as **108**) of the late 15th and early 16th centuries.

Bibliography
Rademacher 1931, p. 294; Rademacher 1933, p. 151, pl. 57c; *Strauss Collection* 1955, p. 39, no. 92; *Phönix aus Sand und Asche* 1988, p. 354, no. 431; Hess and Husband 1997, p. 43, fig. 7A.

107. *BERKEMEYER* WITH STEM AND OPENWORK FOOT

Germany, mid-16th century
H. 11.1 cm, D. (rim) 6.9 cm
Blown; applied
Collection of Karl Amendt, Krefeld (LP 2010-107)

AS **107** and **108** demonstrate, in the early to mid-16th century, several types of drinking vessels were sometimes given short, solid stems and an openwork foot. In this case, the vessel is a *Berkemeyer* similar to **84**. The bowl has two horizontal rows of six prunts, with a continuous rib above them and a "toed" trail at the junction of the wall and the base. The openwork foot was completed by winding a single trail several times around the edge.

Bibliography
Amendt Collection 1987, pp. 79–80, no. 83; *Phönix aus Sand und Asche* 1988, p. 414, no. 520; *Amendt Collection* 2005, p. 154, no. 107.

108. GOBLET WITH OPENWORK FOOT

Probably Germany, probably about 1500–1550
H. 14 cm, D. (rim) 8.2 cm
Blown; applied
The Corning Museum of Glass (79.3.199, gift of The Ruth Bryan Strauss
*   Memorial Foundation)*
Formerly in the Strauss Collection (1370)

THIS is a straight-sided ribbed beaker on a short, solid stem, and with a trailed openwork foot. Ribbed beakers are not uncommon (cf. **38–40**), and openwork feet made by creating a simple network of applied trails are a feature of early to mid-16th-century goblets.

The quality and immaculate condition of the glass have given rise to questions about the authenticity of the object. Apart from its condition, however, the goblet has every appearance of being genuine.

Bibliography
Phönix aus Sand und Asche 1988, pp. 414–415, no. 521.

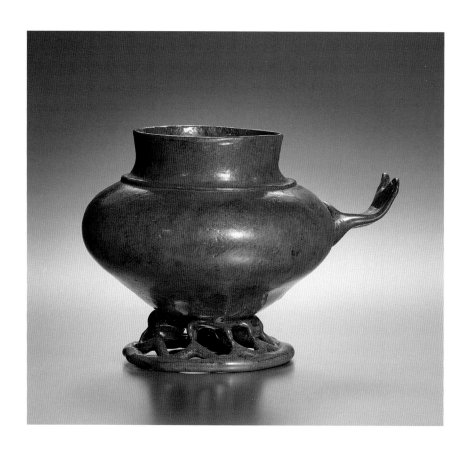

109. *SCHEUER* WITH OPENWORK FOOT

Germany, early 16th century
H. 11 cm, D. (rim) 7.4 cm
Blown; applied
Collection of Karl Amendt, Krefeld (LP 2010-56)

THIS EXAMPLE may have been found in Mainz, Germany.

Bibliography
Phönix aus Sand und Asche 1988, p. 382, no. 475.

110. LID WITH CLAWS AND ANIMALS' HEADS

Germany, first half of the 16th century
H. 18.1 cm, D. (base) 11.6 cm
Blown (two gathers); applied
Collection of Karl Amendt, Krefeld (LP 2010-165)

THE DECORATION of this exceptionally elaborate lid consists of, at the top, an openwork lattice or "cage" composed of four horizontal zigzag trails and, on the side, four long claws above four animal heads. The claws and heads are hollow. They were formed by applying blobs of molten glass to the lid while it was still on the blowpipe. The hot glass softened the side of the lid at the points of contact, enabling the glassmaker to inflate them and tool them to the desired shapes (see page 27).

The object is thought to have been found in Cologne, Germany.

Bibliography
Amendt Collection 2005, pp. 206 and 287, no. 165.

111. BEAKERS WITH GILDED AND ENAMELED DECORATION

Eastern Mediterranean, late 12th to early 13th century
H. 22.3 cm, D. (rim) about 7 cm; H. 22 cm, D. (rim) about 7 cm
Blown; gilded, enameled
The Corning Museum of Glass (67.1.19, .20, gifts of Wilhelm Henrich)

IN 1964 and 1967, the Corning Museum received two groups of fragments that were thought to represent three or four different objects. Subsequently, most of the fragments were reassembled to make two almost identical beakers, presumably a pair or part of a set.

The beakers were decorated with gold (applied in suspension) and enamel, which is now pale yellow. Much of the decoration has been lost, but a sufficient amount remains to show that each beaker has three horizontal rows of roundels. Each row contains three roundels, and each roundel contains a gilded bird with scratched feathers and other details.

The beakers belong to a group of gilded and enameled vessels from sites in the eastern Mediterranean, notably Paphos on Cyprus and Corinth in Greece. Other examples have been found in Italy, the United Kingdom, Sweden, and Belarus.

Bibliography
Whitehouse 2002 (with earlier references).

112. HEDWIG BEAKER

Place of manufacture uncertain, perhaps Sicily,
*   late 12th century*
H. 8.7 cm, D. about 7.1 cm
Blown (perhaps in mold); wheel-cut
The Corning Museum of Glass (67.1.11)

THE BEAKER is decorated with two lions. It was found in the sacristy of St. Stephen's Cathedral in Halberstadt, Germany, in 1820.

Hedwig beakers take their name from Saint Hedwig of Silesia (d. 1243), who is traditionally associated with two of them. The ascetic Hedwig annoyed her husband, Duke Henry I, by refusing to drink wine. According to legend, on one occasion Hedwig was drinking water when Henry snatched the glass from her, only to find that the water had turned into wine.

The earliest datable Hedwig beakers belong to the late 12th or early 13th century, and this is probably the date of the beakers that cannot be closely dated. Thirteen Hedwig beakers survived in medieval European treasuries, and fragments of others have been found in archeological excavations in various parts of Europe. Not a single example has been reported from the Islamic world. Nevertheless, no other cut glass is known to have been made in Europe during the Middle Ages, and the origin of the Hedwig beakers remains uncertain (but see page 52).

Bibliography
Phönix aus Sand und Asche 1988, pp. 95–97, no. 40 (with earlier references); Lierke 2005, pp. 97–98; Whitehouse 2010, pp. 333–337.

113. THE CUP OF CHARLEMAGNE

Probably Syria, late 12th to early 13th century
H. 15 cm, D. 14.7 cm; with mount: H. 24 cm
Blown; gilded, enameled
Musée des Beaux-Arts, Chartres (5144)

ACCORDING TO LEGEND, this beaker was presented by Hārūn al-Rashīd, caliph of Baghdad (r. 786–809), to Charlemagne, who donated it to the abbey of the Madeleine at Châteaudun, Eure-et-Loire, France. Although the legend is false, the gilded copper mount is French and of the 14th century, and it proves that the beaker was already in Europe in the Middle Ages.

The band of geometric decoration on a background of dots is similar to the decoration on the Cup of the Eight Priests, an Islamic gilded and enameled beaker, which was donated to the cathedral of Douai, France, in 1329 and disappeared during World War I. The inscription on the Cup of Charlemagne is similar in style to that on the Palmer Cup, a late 12th- to early 13th-century beaker in The British Museum, London (Contadini 1998; Tait 1998).

The Cup of Charlemagne shares with the Cup of the Eight Priests, the Palmer Cup, and several other Islamic gilded and enameled beakers an otherwise unrecorded method of forming the base, which created on the inside an air-filled dome with a dimple at the center (Tait 1998; Tait 1999, pp. 93–97). It is reasonable to suppose that all beakers with this type of base were made in the same region, possibly at approximately the same time.

Bibliography
A travers le verre 1989, p. 191, no. 123 (with earlier references).

114. BEAKER WITH POLO PLAYERS

Probably Syria, mid-13th century
H. 15.5 cm, D. 10.5 cm
Blown; gilded, enameled
Musée du Louvre, Paris (A.O. 6131)

THIS ISLAMIC drinking vessel is said to have been found beneath an altar in the Church of Santa Margherita at Orvieto, a city in the Umbria region of central Italy, when the building was demolished in 1897. There was no metal mount, which might have turned the beaker into a chalice (like the mounts on other Islamic gilded and enameled vessels and on several Hedwig beakers), and—if the reported find-place is correct—one can only conjecture that it was kept in the church because it contained a relic or was revered in its own right as a treasure from the Holy Land.

The decoration, however, is entirely secular. Between two bands of inscription in the cursive *nashki* script is a scene in which three galloping horsemen are separated by large vegetal scrolls. The horsemen wear turbans and ankle-length robes. They are playing polo, a team sport played on horseback, which originated in Iran more than 2,000 years ago. Similar scenes, with three polo-playing horsemen wearing turbans, appear on a glass beaker in the Grünes Gewölbe (Green Vault) of the Staatliche Kunstsammlungen Dresden, Germany, and on a pitcher in a private collection (*Batsheva de Rothschild Collection* 2000, pp. 58–65, lot 15).

Bibliography
L'Orient de Saladin 2001, p. 191, no. 204 (with earlier references).

115. BEAKER REUSED AS A MONSTRANCE

Probably Syria, 14th century (glass); Italy, 14th century (mount)
H. 7.9 cm, D. 5.7 cm; with mount: H. 42.2 cm
Blown; enameled
LVR-Landesmuseum Bonn (203)

IN Roman Catholic churches, a monstrance is a vessel in which the consecrated Host or sacred relics are displayed. This example consists of a glass container in a gilded bronze mount.

The container is the bottom of a beaker decorated with a vegetal scroll outlined in red enamel. When new, the decoration was probably gilded, but (if so) all trace of gilding has disappeared. The style of the decoration indicates that the beaker was made in the Islamic world, probably Syria, in the 14th century.

The mount consists of a cover and a base. The conical cover is surmounted by a crucifix. The base has a hexagonal stem with a knop just above the midpoint, and a flat hexagonal foot. The mount was made in northern Italy in the 14th century, soon after the beaker arrived in Europe.

Bibliography
Phönix aus Sand und Asche 1988, pp. 124–125, no. 71 (with earlier references); Shalem 1996, p. 245, no. 108.

116. RELIQUARY

(not illustrated)

Probably Italy, date unknown
H. (container) 5.2–5.5 cm, (cover) 6.1 cm; D. (container, rim) 6.9 cm
Blown
Museo Sacro of the Biblioteca Apostolica Vaticana, Vatican City (60333)

116 AND **117** are two of seven similar reliquaries found in an altar in the Church of San Giorgio in Velabro, Rome. The existing church was built during the pontificate of Leo II (682–683). It was restored by Gregory IV (r. 827–844) and enlarged in the 13th century. Fremersdorf (see below) identified the reliquaries as Venetian, probably of the 11th to 12th centuries. However, neither the place of manufacture nor the date of these objects has been established.

Bibliography
Fremersdorf 1975, p. 104, no. 946.

117. RELIQUARY

(not illustrated)

Probably Italy, date unknown
H. (container) 3.5–3.9 cm, (cover) 4.8 cm; D. (container, max.) 4.4 cm
Blown
Museo Sacro of the Biblioteca Apostolica Vaticana, Vatican City (60330)

See **116**.

Bibliography
Fremersdorf 1975, p. 104, no. 943.

118.   CUCURBIT

Germany, perhaps 15th century
H. 14.4 cm, D. (max.) 6.7 cm
Blown
Collection of Karl Amendt, Krefeld (LP 2010-160)

THE DISTINCTIVE gourdlike shape makes the identification of this vessel as a cucurbit certain. The cucurbit (Latin *cucurbita*, "gourd") was one of the three basic components of a medieval distilling apparatus, described on pages 58–59, the other parts being the alembic, which was placed above the cucurbit, and the receiver. Liquid was boiled in the cucurbit, the resultant vapor was trapped and condensed in the alembic, and the distillate was collected in the receiver. As Moorhouse (1972, p. 102) observed: "It is extremely rare for glass cucurbits to survive in archaeological contexts. They suffer the same fate as any thin glass vessel in that, when smashed, they are virtually beyond repair, and only the more durable pieces like the rim and bottom survive."

This cucurbit was probably found in Mainz, Germany.

Bibliography
Amendt Collection 2005, pp. 201 and 286, no. 160.

119. ALEMBIC

Possibly Islamic, date uncertain
L. 12.4 cm, D. (condenser) 7.2 cm, (rim) 3.3 cm
Blown (two gathers)
The Corning Museum of Glass (63.1.6)

DURING the medieval period, many scientific experiments depended on glass apparatus that was transparent and did not contaminate its contents by corroding.

No apparatus played a more important role in these experiments than the still that was used for preparing acids and distilling alcohol. Apart from a source of heat, most medieval stills consisted of three elements, which were developed in the Islamic world and transmitted to Europe. The liquid awaiting distillation was heated in a flask known as the cucurbit (**118**). On top of the cucurbit was a vessel designed to trap the vapor that rose from the boiling liquid. This was the alembic (from the Arabic word *al-anbiq*, "still"). The vapor condensed in the alembic, and the condensate, which ran down the spout of the alembic, was caught in the third element, the receiver.

120. ALEMBIC

Presumably Europe, date uncertain
L. 22.9 cm, D. (opening at base) 6.2 cm
The Corning Museum of Glass (80.3.12)

THE STILL was among the basic apparatus of scientists in the early Islamic world and in medieval and early modern Europe. In the course of a thousand years, the three elements of the still—the cucurbit (**118**), the alembic, and the receiver—changed very little. This alembic, probably made in Europe in the last 500 years, is identical in form and function to **119**, which may have been made centuries earlier in the Near East.

Bibliography
Glass of the Alchemists 2008, p. 141, no. 1.

Glass in the Renaissance

Late 15th to Early 16th Centuries

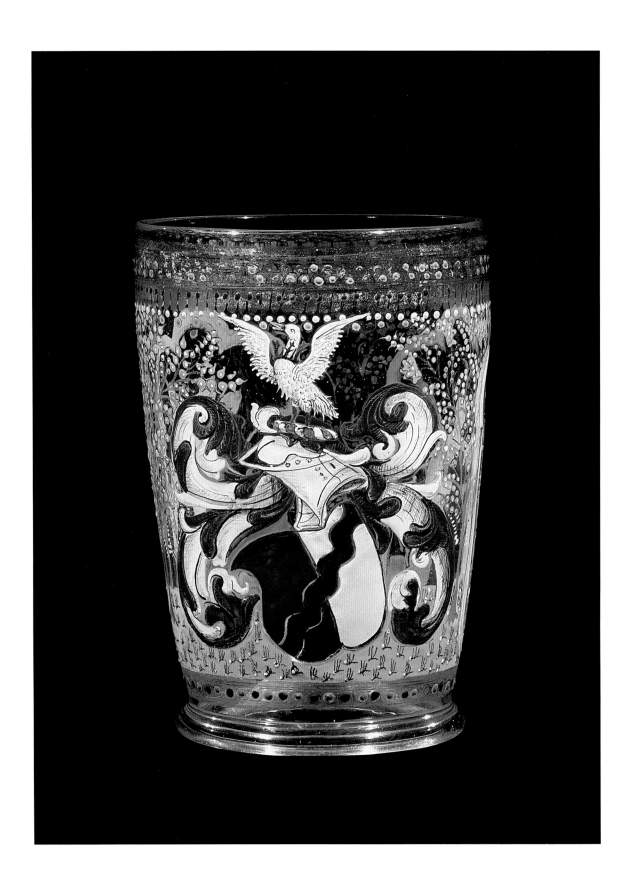

121. THE BEHAIM BEAKER

Venice, probably 1495
H. 10.7 cm, D. (rim) 7.3 cm
Blown; gilded, enameled
The Corning Museum of Glass (84.3.24)

THIS IS an outstanding, and probably datable, early example of Venetian *cristallo* (see page 85), and it demonstrates how glass from Venice was sought after abroad. The beaker is decorated with a coat of arms and two figures. The arms are those of the patrician Behaim family of Nuremberg, Germany. One of the figures is the archangel Michael, who is shown killing a dragon (which represents Satan); the second figure is Saint Catherine of Alexandria.

The combination of Michael and Catherine is without precedent, and the arms of the Behaim family suggest why they should appear together. On July 7, 1495, Michael Behaim married Katerina Lochnerin, the daughter of a wealthy Nuremberg merchant with extensive business interests in Venice.

The beaker, it is believed, was one of a set of souvenir glasses made for the bride and groom, or for important guests at the marriage banquet.

Bibliography
Beyond Venice 2004, pp. iii–iv.

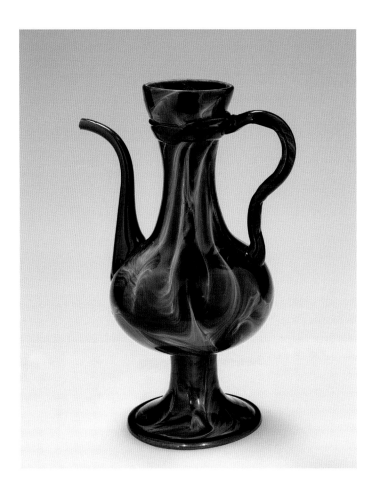

122. EWER

Venice, about 1500–1525
H. 29.9 cm
Blown (two gathers); applied
The Corning Museum of Glass (2001.3.56, gift of Robert and Deborah Truitt)

THIS IS an example of Venetian *calcedonio*, a variety of glass marbled with brown, blue, green, and yellow swirls in imitation of the hard stone chalcedony, which is a form of banded agate. *Calcedonio* was produced in the workshop of Angelo Barovier (1405–1460), the most celebrated Venetian glassmaker of the 15th century, after which it remained in production for more than 200 years, and it was revived in the 19th century. Writing of Venice in 1500, Marcantonio Sabellico noted that "there is no kind of precious stone that cannot be imitated by the industry of the glass-workers." However, *calcedonio* was difficult to make, and it was never common.

Bibliography
Beyond Venice 2004, pp. 7–8.

123. JUG WITH THE COAT OF ARMS OF A MEDICI POPE

Venice, 1513–1534
H. 19.7 cm, D. (max.) 17 cm
Blown; applied, gilded, enameled
The Corning Museum of Glass (2005.3.28)

THE FORM and the decoration indicate that this object was made in the early 16th century. The coat of arms is that of the Medici family, which ruled Florence between 1434 and 1743. It is associated with crossed keys and a papal tiara. This combination suggests that the person for whom the jug was made was a Medici pope. Two members of the Medici family were popes in the early 16th century: Giovanni, who reigned as Pope Leo X in 1513–1521, and Giulio, who reigned as Clement VII in 1523–1534. The jug and other vessels from the same set were probably made for Leo X, a major patron of the arts, who enjoyed a sumptuous lifestyle.

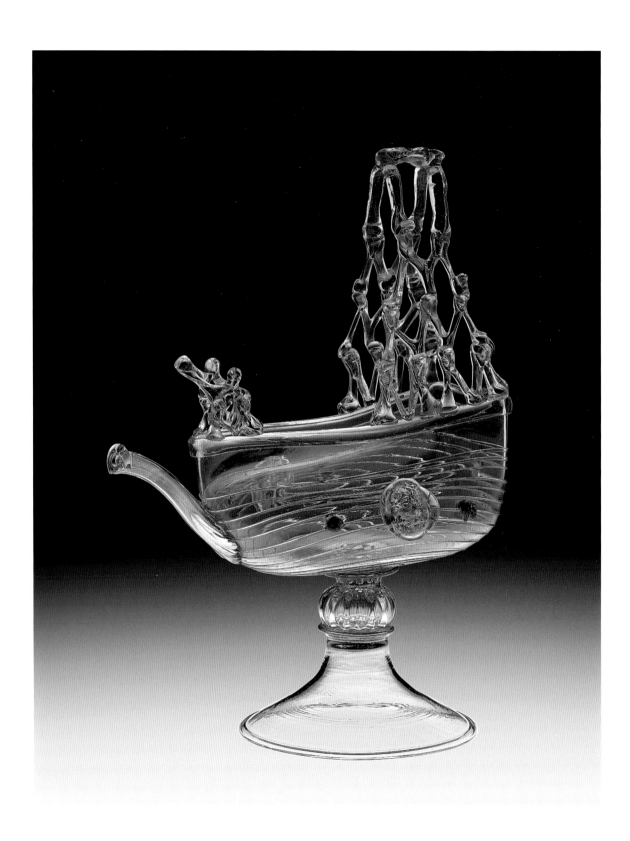

124. NEF

Venice, about 1550–1600
H. 27.3 cm, L. 20.3 cm
Blown (knop blown in dip mold); applied, stamped, gilded
The Corning Museum of Glass (2009.3.8, purchased in part with funds
from the F. M. Kirby Foundation)

A NEF (from Old French *nef*, "ship") is an elaborate table ornament or pouring vessel in the form of a boat. The most sumptuous late medieval and Renaissance nefs are of gold or silver. According to tradition, the earliest glass nefs were made in Venice by Ermonia Vivarini about 1521. In this example, the hull and the trumpet-shaped foot were blown from separate bubbles of glass, and the rigging was constructed from a series of trails. The hull is decorated with gilded lion masks and blue prunts. The presence of a spout shows that the object could be used for pouring wine or other liquids. Nefs without spouts could be employed as containers for pepper and spices, or for cutlery.

Bibliography
Notable Acquisitions 2010.

125. EWER

Spain, Catalonia, about 1475–1550
H. 23.8 cm
Blown (two gathers), mold-blown; applied
The Corning Museum of Glass (2008.3.15)

VENETIAN GLASS was sought after all over Europe between the 15th and 17th centuries. From Austria to Spain, local glassmakers produced glass *à la façon de Venise*: glass made in the Venetian manner. The glassmakers of Barcelona were among the earliest imitators of Venetian glass in Spain, and while some of their products are difficult to distinguish from Venetian glasses, others display a distinctive local flavor.

This ewer, for example, is unlike vessels made in Venice, although its maker used techniques perfected by Venetian glassworkers.

It was blown from two bubbles of deep blue glass. The body has a pattern of mold-blown ribs pinched to form a lattice pattern known as "nipt-diamond-waies." The foot also has mold-blown ribs, and the ribs on both the body and the foot have broken white trails. The handle has pinched, earlike decorations, and there is similar decoration on the spout, which also has a white lip wrap.

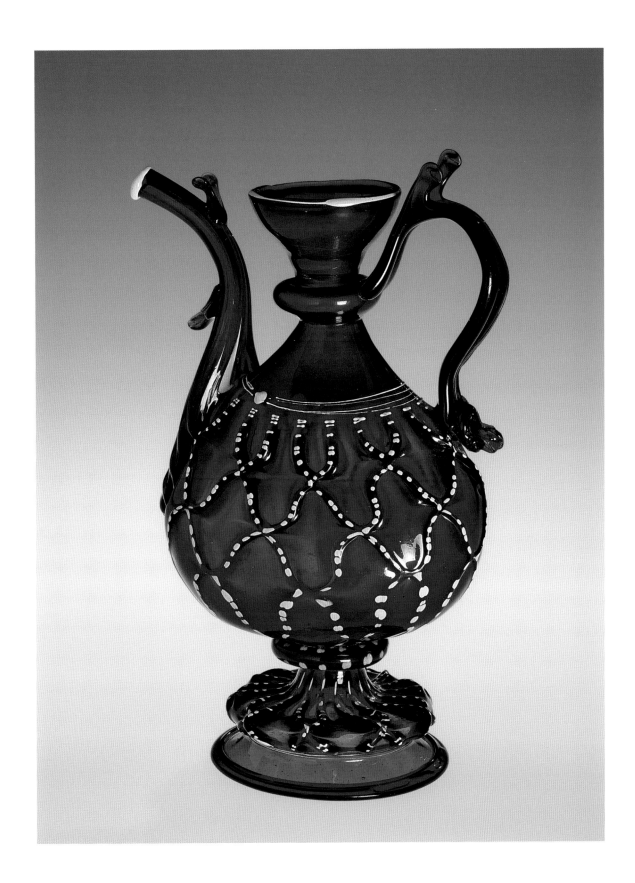

126. EWER WITH MILLEFIORI DECORATION

Spain, Catalonia, about 1550–1600
H. 24.9 cm
Mold-blown (two gathers); applied, gilded, tooled
The Corning Museum of Glass (2003.3.70, purchased in part
*   with funds from the Houghton Endowment)*
Formerly in the collection of Christopher Fish

THE BUBBLES of molten glass that formed the body and foot of the vessel were partly inflated in a dip mold to create the vertical ribs, which are more prominent on the foot than on the body. The decoration, known as millefiori (Italian, "1,000 flowers"), was made by rolling the bubbles on a surface strewn with pieces of canes (multicolored glass rods that were bundled and fused to form a polychrome design).

The pieces stuck to the semimolten bubbles. As the glassblower continued to inflate the bubbles, many of the fragments, particularly those at the midsection of the body, became stretched. This is the only known example of a ewer of this shape with millefiori decoration.

Bibliography
Beyond Venice 2004, p. 128, no. 8.

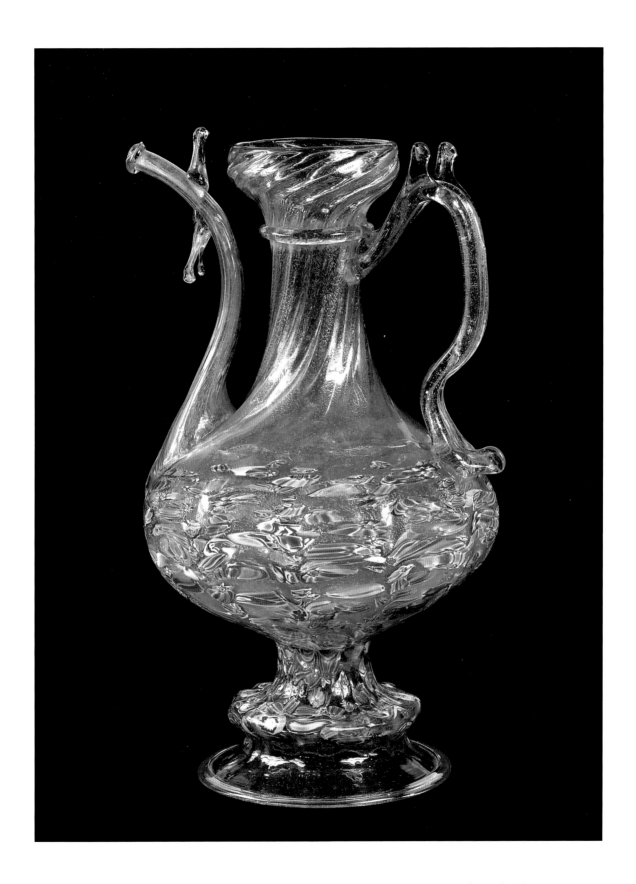

127. DRAGON-STEM GOBLET

Possibly Venice, 17th century
H. 26.2 cm, D. (rim) 7.7 cm
Blown (some parts in dip mold); applied
The Corning Museum of Glass (51.3.118)

IN AND AFTER the second half of the 15th century, Venetian glassmakers made frequent use of canes composed of colorless and opaque white glass, sometimes accompanied or replaced by blue or red. Elsewhere in Europe, similar canes became one of the hallmarks of glass produced *à la façon de Venise*. In this dragon-stem goblet, the body of the creature was formed from a cane of colorless glass with a red twist.

It is sometimes difficult to determine whether such vessels were made in Venice or some other part of Europe, perhaps by an emigrant Venetian glass master.

Bibliography
Beyond Venice 2004, p. v.

128. GOBLET

France, early 16th century
H. 14.8 cm
Blown (two gathers), mold-blown; enameled
The Corning Museum of Glass (72.3.52, acquired from A. Vecht, Amsterdam)

THE LOWER PART of the bowl was blown in a dip mold with 12 vertical ribs. The inscription, in French, is "POVRMOSVRLELEOTE-NÂTRENALDI" (probably For Monsieur the Lieutenant Trenaldi). Beneath the inscription, the decoration consists of two dogs and a stag painted in white and dark brown enamel.

Bibliography
Beyond Venice 2004, p. 172, no. 5.

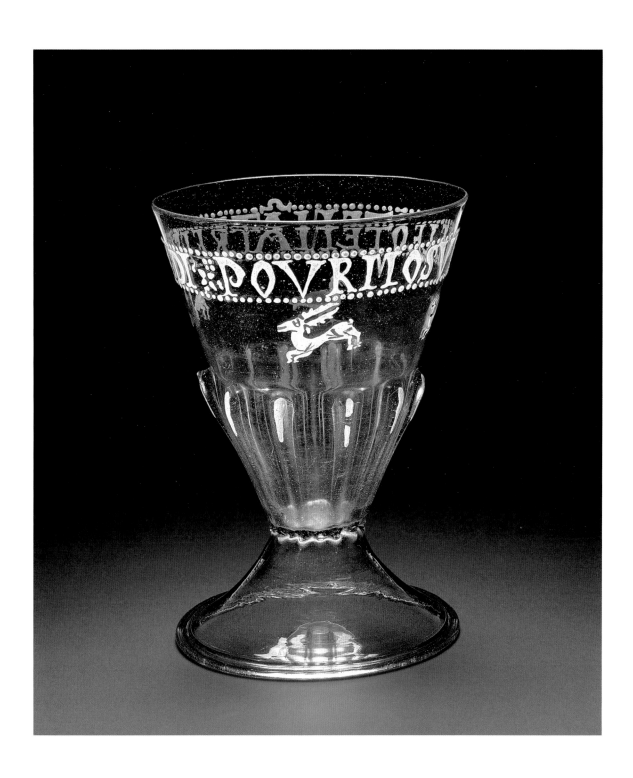

Bibliography

MOST WORKS are cited by author(s) and date of publication (e.g., Shalem 1996). Exhibition catalogs are cited by name and date (e.g., *Phönix aus Sand und Asche* 1988). Catalogs (including sale catalogs) of well-known private collections are cited by owner's name and date (e.g., *Amendt Collection* 1987).

Works preceded by an asterisk (∗) are relatively general studies that would provide the reader with more information on the subject of medieval glass.

The following abbreviations are used in the bibliography and in the text:

A. NAMES OF PUBLICATIONS

AnnAIHV	Annales de l'Association Internationale pour l'Histoire du Verre
JGS	Journal of Glass Studies

B. OTHER

ed.	edited by, editor
edn.	edition
fig., figs.	figure, figures
fol.	folio
inv.	inventory
n.	note
no., nos.	number, numbers
p., pp.	page, pages
pl.	plate
pt.	part
rev.	revised
trans.	translator
v	verso
v., vv.	volume, volumes

∗ *A travers le verre* 1989
Danièle Foy and Geneviève Sennequier, *A travers le verre du Moyen Age à la Renaissance*, Rouen: Musées et Monuments Départementaux de la Seine-Maritime, 1989.

Amendt Collection 1987
Erwin Baumgartner, *Glas des späten Mittelalters: Die Sammlung Karl Amendt*, Düsseldorf: Kunstmuseum Düsseldorf, 1987.

∗ *Amendt Collection* 2005
Erwin Baumgartner, *Glas des Mittelalters und der Renaissance: Die Sammlung Karl Amendt = Glass of the Middle Ages and the Renaissance Period: The Karl Amendt Collection*, Düsseldorf: Museum Kunst Palast, Glasmuseum Hentrich, 2005.

Arbman 1940–43
Holger Arbman, *Birka: I. Die Gräbar,* Kungl. Vitterhets Historie och Antikvitets Akademien, Birka Untersuchungen und Studien, I, Uppsala: Almqvist & Wiksells, 2 vv., 1940–1943.

Batsheva de Rothschild Collection 2000
The Collection of the Late Baroness Batsheva de Rothschild, sale catalog, London: Christie's, December 14, 2000.

∗ *Beyond Venice* 2004
Jutta-Annette Page and others, *Beyond Venice: Glass in Venetian Style, 1500–1750*, Corning: The Corning Museum of Glass, 2004.

Brill 1999
Robert H. Brill, *Chemical Analyses of Early Glasses*, v. 1, *Catalogue of Samples*, and v. 2, *Tables of Analyses*, Corning: The Corning Museum of Glass, 1999.

Byzance 1992
Byzance: L'Art byzantin dans les collections publiques françaises, Paris: Editions de la Réunion des Musées Nationaux, 1992.

Cabart 1993
Hubert Cabart, "Les Gobelets mérovingiens à inscription du Musée de Châlons-sur-Marne (France)," *AnnAIHV*, v. 12, Vienna, 1991 (Amsterdam, 1993), pp. 225–233.

Cabart and Feyeux 1995
Hubert Cabart and Jean-Yves Feyeux, *Verres de Champagne: Le Verre à l'époque mérovingienne en Champagne-Ardenne*, Reims, France: Société Archéologique Champenoise, 1995.

Carboni 1998
Stefano Carboni, "Gregorio's Tale; or, Of Enamelled Glass Production in Venice," in *Gilded and Enamelled Glass from the Middle East*, ed. Rachel Ward, London: British Museum Press, 1998, pp. 101–106.

Carboni 2001
Stefano Carboni, *Glass from Islamic Lands*, New York: Thames & Hudson in association with the al-Sabah Collection, Dar al-Athar al-Islamiyyah, Kuwait National Museum, 2001.

Carboni, Lacerenza, and Whitehouse 2003
Stefano Carboni, Giancarlo Lacerenza, and David Whitehouse, "Glassmaking in Medieval Tyre: The Written Evidence," *JGS*, v. 45, 2003, pp. 139–149.

Contadini 1998
Anna Contadini, "Poetry on Enamelled Glass: The Palmer Cup in the British Museum," in *Gilded and Enamelled Glass from the Middle East*, ed. Rachel Ward, London: British Museum, 1998, pp. 56–60.

Cradle of Christianity 2000
Yael Israeli and David Mevorah, ed., *Cradle of Christianity*, Jerusalem: Israel Museum, 2000.

Davidson 1952
Gladys R. Davidson, *Corinth: Results of Excavations Conducted by the American School of Classical Studies at Athens*, v. 12, *The Minor Objects*, Princeton, New Jersey: the school, 1952.

Dell'Acqua 1997
Francesca Dell'Acqua, "Ninth-Century Window Glass from the Monastery of San Vincenzo al Volturno (Molise, Italy)," *JGS*, v. 39, 1997, pp. 33–41.

Dillon 1907
Edward Dillon, *Glass*, New York: G. P. Putnam, and London: Methuen, 1907.

Distelberger 2004
Rudolf Distelberger, "Die Gefässe aus Bergkristall," in *Nobiles Officinae: Die königlichen Hofwerkstätten zu Palermo zur Zeit der Normannen und Staufer im 12. und 13. Jahrhundert*, ed. Wilfried Seipel, Milan: Skira, 2004, pp. 109–113.

Distelberger 2005
Rudolf Distelberger, "Die Hedwigsbecher und die Steinschneidekunst," in Rosemarie Lierke, *Die Hedwigsbecher: Das normannisch-sizilische Erbe der staufischen Kaiser,* Mainz: Rutzen, 2005, pp. 83–94.

Dobkin Collection 2003
Yael Israeli, with contributions by Dan Barag and Na'ama Brosh, *Ancient Glass in the Israel Museum: The Eliahu Dobkin Collection and Other Gifts*, Jerusalem: the museum, 2003.

Effros 2005
Bonnie Effros, "Art of the 'Dark Ages': Showing Merovingian Artefacts in North American Public and Private Collections," *Journal of the History of Collections*, v. 17, no. 1, 2005, pp. 85–113.

Eisen 1927
Gustavus A. Eisen, assisted by Fahim Kouchakji, *Glass: Its Origin, History, Chronology, Technic and Classification to the Sixteenth Century*, 2 vv., New York: W. E. Rudge, 1927.

Evison 1975
Vera I. Evison, "Germanic Glass Drinking Horns," *JGS*, v. 17, 1975, pp. 74–87.

Evison 2008
Vera I. Evison, with contributions from Ian C. Freestone, Michael J. Hughes, and Colleen P. Stapleton, *Catalogue of Anglo-Saxon Glass in the British Museum*, ed. Sonja Marzinzik, Research Publications, no. 167, London: the museum, 2008.

Feyeux 1995
Jean-Yves Feyeux, "La Typologie de la verrerie mérovingienne du nord de la France," in *Le Verre de l'Antiquité tardive et du Haut Moyen Age*, ed. Danièle Foy, Guiry-en-Vexin: Musée Archéologique Départemental du Val d'Oise, 1995, pp. 109–137.

Feyeux 2003
Jean-Yves Feyeux, *Le Verre mérovingien du quart nord-est de la France*, Paris: De Boccard, 2003.

Follman-Schulz 1995
Anna-Barbara Follman-Schulz, "A propos des précurseurs romains du *Rüsselbecher*," in *Le Verre de l'Antiquité tardive et du haut Moyen Age: Typologie, chronologie, diffusion*, ed. Danièle Foy, Association Française pour l'Archéologie du Verre, 8ème Rencontre, Guiry-en-Vexin, France: Musée Archéologique Départemental du Val d'Oise, 1995, pp. 85–92.

Foy 1985
Danièle Foy, "Essai de typologie des verres médiévaux d'après les fouilles provençales et languedociennes," *JGS*, v. 27, 1985, pp. 18–71.

Foy and Démians d'Archimbaud 1996
Danièle Foy and Gabrielle Démians d'Archimbaud, "Dépôts de verres et rites funéraires," in *Archéologie du cimetière chrétien: Actes du 2ᵉ colloque A.R.C.H.E.A.* [Association en Région Centre pour l'Histoire et l'Archéologie], *Orléans, . . . 1994*, Tours, 1996, pp. 225–241.

Freestone 2003
Ian C. Freestone, "Primary Glass Sources in the Mid First Millennium AD," *AnnAIHV*, v. 15, New York and Corning, 2001 (Nottingham, 2003), pp. 111–115.

Freestone, Gudenrath, and Cartwright 2008
Ian C. Freestone, William Gudenrath, and Caroline Cartwright, "The Hope Goblet Reconsidered. I. Technological Considerations," *JGS*, v. 50, 2008, pp. 159–169.

Fremersdorf 1975
Fritz Fremersdorf, *Antikes, islamisches und mittel-alterliches Glas sowie kleinere Arbeiten aus Stein, Gagat und verwandten Stoffen in den vatikanischen Sammlungen Roms . . .* , Catalogo del Museo Sacro della Biblioteca Apostolica Vaticana, v. 5, Vatican City: the library, 1975.

Gasparetto 1975
Astone Gasparetto, "La Verrerie vénitienne et ses relations avec le Levant balkanique au moyen âge," *Srednjovekovno staklo na Balkanu: V–XV vek: Sbornik radova sa međunarodnog savetovanja održanog od 22. do 24. aprila 1974. u Beogradu = Verre médiéval aux Balkans (V^e–XVe)*, Beograd: Balkanološki Institut Srpske Akademije Nauka i Umetnosti, 1975, pp. 143–155.

Gerth, Wedepohl, and Heide 1998
K. Gerth, K. H. Wedepohl, and K. Heide, "Experimental Melts to Explore the Technique of Medieval Woodash Glass Production and the Chlorine Content of Medieval Glass Types," *Chemie der Erde*, v. 58, no. 3, 1998, pp. 219–232.

Glass from the Ancient World 1957
Glass from the Ancient World: The Ray Winfield Smith Collection, Corning: The Corning Museum of Glass, 1957.

Glass of the Alchemists 2008
Dedo von Kerssenbrock-Krosigk and others, *Glass of the Alchemists: Lead Crystal–Gold Ruby, 1650–1750*, Corning: The Corning Museum of Glass, 2008.

* *Glass of the Caesars* 1987
Donald B. Harden and others, *Glass of the Caesars*, Milan: Olivetti, 1987.

* *Glass of the Sultans* 2001
Stefano Carboni and David Whitehouse, with contributions by Robert H. Brill and William Gudenrath, *Glass of the Sultans*, New York: The Metropolitan Museum of Art in collaboration with The Corning Museum of Glass, Benaki Museum, and Yale University Press, 2001.

Goethert-Polaschek 1977
Karin Goethert-Polaschek, *Katalog der römischen Gläser des Rheinischen Landesmuseums Trier*, Trierer Grabungen und Forschungen, v. 9, Mainz am Rhein: Philipp von Zabern, 1977.

Gratuze and Barrandon 1990
B. Gratuze and J.-N. Barrandon, "Islamic Glass Weights and Stamps: Analysis Using Nuclear Techniques," *Archaeometry*, v. 32, pt. 2, August 1990, pp. 155–162.

Grose 1977
David F. Grose, "Early Blown Glass: The Western Evidence," *JGS*, v. 19, 1977, pp. 9–29.

Gudenrath 1991
William Gudenrath, "Techniques of Glassmaking and Decoration," in *Five Thousand Years of Glass*, ed. Hugh Tait, London: British Museum Press, 1991, pp. 213–241.

Gudenrath 2001
William Gudenrath, "A Survey of Islamic Glass-working and Glass-Decorating Techniques," in Stefano Carboni and David Whitehouse, with contributions by Robert H. Brill and William Gudenrath, *Glass of the Sultans*, New York: The Metropolitan Museum of Art in association with The Corning Museum of Glass, Benaki Museum, and Yale University Press, 2001, pp. 46–67.

Guide to the Collections 2001
The Corning Museum of Glass: A Guide to the Collections, Corning: the museum, 2001.

Harden 1956
Donald B. Harden, "Glass Vessels in Britain and Ireland, A.D. 400–1000," in *Dark-Age Britain: Studies Presented to E. T. Leeds*, ed. D. B. Harden, London: Methuen & Co. Ltd., 1956, pp. 132–167.

Hartshorne 1897
Albert Hartshorne, *Old English Glasses: An Account of Glass Drinking Vessels in England, from Early Times to the End of the Eighteenth Century*, London and New York: E. Arnold, 1897.

* Henkes 1994
Harold E. Henkes, *Glas zonder glans: Vijf eeuwen gebruiksglas uit de bodem van de Lage Landen 1300–1800 = Glass without Gloss: Utility Glass from Five Centuries Excavated in the Low Countries, 1300–1800*, Rotterdam Papers, no. 9, Rotterdam: Coördinatie Commissie van Advies inzake Archeologisch Onderzoek binnen het Ressort Rotterdam, 1994.

Hess and Husband 1997
Catherine Hess and Timothy Husband, *European Glass in The J. Paul Getty Museum*, Los Angeles: the museum, 1997.

Howard 2000
Deborah Howard, *Venice & the East: The Impact of the Islamic World on Venetian Architecture, 1100–1500*, New Haven: Yale University Press, 2000.

Hunter and Heyworth 1998
J. R. Hunter and M. P. Heyworth, *The Hamwic Glass*, Council for British Archaeology Research Report, no. 116, York, U.K.: the council, 1998.

Isings 1957
C. Isings, *Roman Glass from Dated Finds*, Archaeologica Traiectina, v. 2, Groningen: J. B. Wolters, 1957.

Isings 1980
Clasina Isings, "Glass Finds from Dorestadt, Hoogstraat I," in *Excavations at Dorestadt*, v. 1, *The Harbour: Hoogstraat I*, ed. W. A. Van Es and W. J. H. Verwers, Nederlandse Oudheden 9, Amersfoort: Rijksdienst voor het Oudheidkundig Bodemonderzoek, 1980, pp. 225–237.

Jackson and Smedley 2004
C. M. Jackson and J. W. Smedley, "Medieval and Post-Medieval Glass Technology: Melting Characteristics of Some Glasses Melted from Vegetable Ash and Sand Mixtures," *Glass Technology*, v. 45, no. 1, February 2004, pp. 36–42.

Kojić and Wenzel 1967
Ljubinka Kojić and Marian Wenzel, "Medieval Glass Found in Yugoslavia," *JGS*, v. 9, 1967, pp. 76–93.

Kramarovsky 1998
Mark Kramarovsky, "The Import and Manufacture of Glass in the Territories of the Golden Horde," in *Gilded and Enamelled Glass from the Middle East*, ed. Rachel Ward, London: British Museum, 1998, pp. 96–100.

Kraus and Sauer 1897
Franz Xaver Kraus and Joseph Sauer, *Geschichte der christlichen Kunst*, v. 2, pt. 1, *Die Kunst des Mittelalters, der Renaissance und der Neuzeit Erste Abtheilung*, Freiburg im Breisgau: Herder, 1897.

Križanac 2001
Milica Križanac, *Medieval Glass from the Cathedral of St. Tripun at Kotor*, University of Belgrade, Faculty of Philosophy, Center for Archeological Research, v. 21, Belgrade: the center, 2001 (in Serbian, with English summary).

Kröger 2006
J. Kröger, "The Hedwig Beakers: Medieval European Glass Vessels Made in Sicily around 1200," in *The Phenomenon of "Foreign" in Oriental Art*, ed. A. Hagedorn, Wiesbaden: Reichert, 2006, pp. 27–46.

Krueger 2002
Ingeborg Krueger, "A Second Aldrevandin Beaker and an Update on a Group of Enameled Glasses," *JGS*, v. 44, 2002, pp. 111–132.

Krueger 2008
Ingeborg Krueger, "The Hope Goblet Reconsidered. II. An Art Historian's View," *JGS*, v. 50, 2008, pp. 171–178.

Kunina 1997
Nina Kunina, *Ancient Glass in the Hermitage Collection*, St. Petersburg: State Hermitage and ARS Publishers, 1997.

Lamm 1929–30
C. J. (Carl Johan) Lamm, *Mittelalterliche Gläser und Steinschnittarbeiten aus dem Nahen Osten*, 2 vv., Forschungen zur islamischen Kunst, v. 5, Berlin: D. Reimer, 1929–1930.

Lanmon 1993
Dwight P. Lanmon with David B. Whitehouse, *The Robert Lehman Collection*, v. 11, *Glass*, New York: The Metropolitan Museum of Art, 1993.

Lierke 2005
Rosemarie Lierke, with a contribution by Rudolf Distelberger, *Die Hedwigsbecher: Das normannisch-sizilische Erbe der staufischen Kaiser*, Mainz: Rutzen, 2005.

L'Orient de Saladin 2001
L'Orient de Saladin: L'Art des Ayyoubides, Paris: Institut du Monde Arabe and Gallimard, 2001.

Lusuardi Siena and Zuech 2000
Silvia Lusuardi Siena and Roberta Zuech, "Una lampada di tipo islamico dal *castrum* di Ragogna (Udine, Friuli)," *AnnAIHV*, v. 14, Venice and Milan, 1998 (Lochem, 2000), pp. 243–247.

* Macfarlane and Martin 2002
Alan Macfarlane and Gerry Martin, *Glass: A World History*, Chicago: University of Chicago Press, 2002.

Macquet 1990
Cécile Macquet, "Les Lissoirs de verre, approche technique et bibliographique. Note à l'occasion de l'étude des exemplaires découverts à Saint-Denis," *Archéologie Médiévale*, v. 20, 1990, pp. 319–334.

Masterpieces of Germanic Glass 1979
Rudolf von Strasser, *Masterpieces of Germanic Glass, 15th–19th Centuries*, Neenah, Wisconsin: John Nelson Bergstrom Art Center and Museum, 1979.

* McCray 1999
W. Patrick McCray, *Glassmaking in Renaissance Venice: The Fragile Craft*, Aldershot, U.K., and Brookfield, Vermont: Ashgate, 1999.

Mille anni 1982
Rosa Barovier Mentasti and others, *Mille anni di arte del vetro a Venezia*, 2nd edn., Venice: Albrizzi, 1982.

Moorhouse 1972
Stephen Moorhouse, "Medieval Distilling-Apparatus of Glass and Pottery," *Medieval Archaeology*, v. 16, 1972, pp. 79–121.

Nenna 2000

Marie-Dominique Nenna, ed., *La Route du verre: Ateliers primaires et secondaires du second millénaire av. J.-C. au Moyen Age*, Travaux de la Maison de l'Orient Méditerranéen, no. 33, Lyons: Maison de l'Orient Méditerranéen–Jean Pouilloux, 2000.

Nenna, Picon, and Vichy 2000

Marie-Dominique Nenna, Maurice Picon, and Michèle Vichy, "Ateliers primaires et secondaires en Egypte à l'époque gréco-romaine," in *La Route du verre*: *Ateliers primaires et secondaires du second millénaire av. J.-C. au Moyen Age*, Travaux de la Maison de l'Orient Méditerranéen, no. 33, Lyons: Maison de l'Orient Méditerranéen–Jean Pouilloux, 2000, pp. 97–112.

Newby 1999

Martine S. Newby, "Form and Function of Central Italian Medieval Glass in the Light of Finds from the Benedictine Abbey of Farfa and the Palazzo Vitelleschi at Tarquinia," M. Phil. thesis, University of Durham, United Kingdom, 1999.

Newby 2000

Martine S. Newby, "Some Comparisons in the Form and Function of Glass from Medieval Ecclesiastical and Domestic Sites in Central Italy," *AnnAIHV*, v. 14, Venice and Milan, 1998 (Lochem, 2000), pp. 258–264.

Notable Acquisitions 2010

The Corning Museum of Glass: Notable Acquisitions of 2009, Corning: the museum, forthcoming 2010.

Philippe 1970

Joseph Philippe, *Le Monde byzantin dans l'histoire de la verrerie (V^e–XVIe siècle)*, Bologna: R. Pàtron, 1970.

Philippe 1975

Joseph Philippe, *L'Orient chrétien et des reliquaires médiévaux en cristal de roche et en verre conservés en Belgique*, Liège: Musée du Verre, 1975.

* *Phönix aus Sand und Asche* 1988

Erwin Baumgartner and Ingeborg Krueger, *Phönix aus Sand und Asche: Glas des Mittelalters*, Munich: Klinkhardt & Biermann, 1988.

Picturing the Bible 2007

Jeffrey Spier, ed., *Picturing the Bible: The Earliest Christian Art*, New Haven, Connecticut: Yale University Press in association with the Kimbell Art Museum, 2007.

Pinder-Wilson 1991

Ralph Pinder-Wilson, "The Islamic Lands and China," in *Five Thousand Years of Glass*," ed. Hugh Tait, London: British Museum Press, 1991, pp. 112–143.

Price 2000

Jennifer Price, "Late Roman Glass Vessels in Britain and Ireland from AD 350 to 410 and Beyond," in *Glass in Britain and Ireland, AD 350–1100*, London: British Museum, 2000, pp. 1–31.

Rademacher 1931

Franz Rademacher, "Die Gotischen Gläser der Sammlung Seligmann-Köln," *Pantheon*, v. 8, no. 7, July 1931, pp. 290–294.

Rademacher 1933

Franz Rademacher, *Die deutschen Gläser des Mittelalters*, Berlin: Verlag für Kunstwissenschaft, 1933.

Rademacher 1942

Franz Rademacher, "Fränkische Gläser aus dem Rheinland," *Bonner Jahrbücher*, v. 147, 1942, pp. 285–344.

* *Reflecting Antiquity* 2007

David Whitehouse and others, *Reflecting Antiquity: Modern Glass Inspired by Ancient Rome*, Corning: The Corning Museum of Glass, 2007.

Riis and Poulsen 1957

P. J. Riis and Vagn Poulsen, with E. Hammershaimb, *Hama: Fouilles et recherches de la Fondation Carlsberg, 1931–1938*, v. 4, pt. 2, *Les Verreries et poteries médiévales*, Nationalmuseets Skrifter, Større Beretninger III, Copenhagen: Fondation Carlsberg, 1957.

Ritsema van Eck and Zijlstra-Zweens 1993

Pieter C. Ritsema van Eck and Henrica M. Zijlstra-Zweens, *Glass in the Rijksmuseum*, v. 1, Zwolle: Waanders Uitgevers, 1993.

Royal Hunter 1978

Prudence Oliver Harper, *The Royal Hunter: Art of the Sasanian Empire*, New York: Asia Society in association with John Weatherhill, 1978.

Rückert 1982

Rainer Rückert, *Die Glassammlung des Bayerischen Nationalmuseums München*, Munich: Hirmer, 1982.

Saldern 1996

Axel von Saldern, "Early Islamic Glass in the Near East: Problems of Chronology and Provenances," *AnnAIHV*, v. 13, Pays Bas, 1995 (Lochem, 1996), pp. 225–246.

Sayre 1964

Edward V. Sayre, *Some Ancient Glass Specimens with Compositions of Particular Archaeological Significance*, Upton, New York: Brookhaven National Laboratory, 1964.

Scanlon and Pinder-Wilson 2001

G. T. Scanlon and R. Pinder-Wilson, *Fustat Glass of the Early Islamic Period: Finds Excavated by The*

American Research Center in Egypt, 1964–1980, London: Altajir World of Islam Trust, 2001.

Schmidt 1922

Robert Schmidt, *Das Glas*, 2nd edn., Handbücher der Staatlichen Museen zu Berlin, v. 14, Berlin: Walter de Gruyter, 1922.

Scranton 1957

Robert L. Scranton, *Corinth: Results of Excavations Conducted by the American School of Classical Studies at Athens, v. 16, Mediaeval Architecture in the Central Area of Corinth*, Princeton, New Jersey, the school, 1957.

Shalem 1996

Avinoam Shalem, *Islam Christianized: Islamic Portable Objects in the Medieval Church Treasuries of the Latin West*, Ars Faciendi: Beiträge und Studien zur Kunstgeschichte, v. 7, Frankfurt am Main: Peter Lang, 1996.

Shelkovnikov 1966

B. A. Shelkovnikov, "Russian Glass from the 11th to the 17th Century," *JGS*, v. 8, 1966, pp. 95–115.

Smart and Glasser 1974

R. M. Smart and F. P. Glasser, "Compound Formation and Phase Equilibria in the System PbO-SiO$_2$," *Journal of the American Ceramic Society*, v. 57, no. 9, September 1974, pp. 378–382.

Stevenson 2001

Judith Stevenson, "The Vessel Glass," in *San Vincenzo al Volturno, v. 3, The Finds from the 1980–86 Excavations*, ed. John Mitchell and Inge Lyse Hansen, Spoleto: Centro Italiano di Studi sull'Alto Medioevo, 2001, text, pp. 203–277, illustrations, pp. 223–251.

* Stiaffini 1999

Daniela Stiaffini, *Il vetro nel Medioevo: Tecniche, strutture, manufatti*, Tardoantico e Medioevo. Studi e Strumenti di Archeologia, no. 1, Rome: Fratelli Palombi, 1999.

Strauss Collection 1955

[Jerome Strauss], *Glass Drinking Vessels from the Collections of Jerome Strauss and The Ruth Bryan Strauss Memorial Foundation*, Corning: The Corning Museum of Glass, 1955.

Strong 1966

Donald Emrys Strong, *Greek and Roman Gold and Silver Plate*, London: Methuen, 1966.

Tait 1998

Hugh Tait, "The Palmer Cup and Related Glasses Exported to Europe in the Middle Ages," in *Gilded and Enamelled Glass from the Middle East*, ed. Rachel Ward, London: British Museum Press, 1998, pp. 50–55.

Tait 1999

Hugh Tait, "Venice: Heir to the Glassmakers of Islam or of Byzantium?" in *Islam and the Italian Renaissance*, ed. Charles Burnett and Anna Contadini, Warburg Institute Colloquia, no. 5, London: the institute, 1999, pp. 77–104.

Theophilus 1961

Theophilus, *The Various Arts*, translated from the Latin with introduction and notes by C. R. (Charles Reginald) Dodwell, London and New York: Thomas Nelson and Sons Ltd., 1961.

Toynbee 1903

Paget J. Toynbee, "Dante's References to Glass," *Giornale Storico della Letteratura Italiana*, v. 41, 1903, pp. 78–83.

Tronzo 1997

William Tronzo, *The Cultures of His Kingdom: Roger II and the Cappella Palatina in Palermo*, Princeton, New Jersey: Princeton University Press, 1997.

* Tyson 2000

Rachel Tyson, *Medieval Glass Vessels Found in England, c AD 1200–1500*, Council for British Archaeology Research Report, no. 121, York, U.K.: the council, 2000.

Wedepohl 2003

Karl Hans Wedepohl, *Glas in Antike und Mittelalter: Geschichte eines Werkstoffs*, Stuttgart: Schweizerbart'sche Verlagsbuchhandlung, 2003.

Wedepohl 2005

Karl Hans Wedepohl, *Die Gruppe der Hedwigsbecher*, Nachrichten der Akademie der Wissenschaften zu Göttingen II, 2005, no. 1, Mathematisch-Physikalische Klasse, Göttingen: Vandenhoeck & Reprecht, 2005, no. 1.

Wedepohl, Krueger, and Hartmann 1995

Karl Hans Wedepohl, Ingeborg Krueger, and Gerald Hartmann, "Medieval Lead Glass from Northwestern Europe," *JGS*, v. 37, 1995, pp. 65–82.

Wedepohl, Winkelmann, and Hartmann 1997

Karl Hans Wedepohl, Wilhelm Winkelmann, and Gerald Hartmann, "Glasfunde aus der karolingischen Pfalz in Paderborn und die frühe Holzasche-Glasherstellung," *Ausgrabungen und Funde in Westfalen-Lippe 9A*, 1997, pp. 41–53.

Wedepohl and others 2007

Karl Hans Wedepohl and others, "A Hedwig Beaker Fragment from Brno (Czech Republic)," *JGS*, v. 49, 2007, pp. 266–268.

Wenzel 1984

Marian Wenzel, "13th-Century Islamic Enamelled

Glass Found in Medieval Abingdon," *Oxford Journal of Archaeology*, v. 3, no. 3, 1984, pp. 1–21.

Whitehouse 1986

David Whitehouse, "An Anglo-Saxon Cone Beaker from Faversham," *JGS*, v. 28, 1986, pp. 120–122.

Whitehouse 1987

David Whitehouse, "Medieval Glass from Tarquinia," *AnnAIHV*, v. 10, Madrid and Segovia, 1985 (Amsterdam, 1987), pp. 317–330.

* Whitehouse 1991

David Whitehouse, "Glassmaking at Corinth: A Reassessment," in *Ateliers de verriers de l'Antiquité à la période pré-industrielle*, ed. Danièle Foy and Geneviève Sennequier, Rouen: Association Française pour l'Archéologie du Verre, 1991, pp. 73–82.

Whitehouse 1993

David Whitehouse, "The Date of the 'Agora South Centre' Workshop at Corinth," *Archeologia Medievale*, v. 20, 1993, pp. 659–662.

Whitehouse 1997

David Whitehouse, *Roman Glass in The Corning Museum of Glass*, v. 1, Corning: the museum, 1997.

Whitehouse 1998

David Whitehouse, "Byzantine Gilded Glass," in *Gilded and Enamelled Glass from the Middle East*, ed. Rachel Ward, London: British Museum Press, 1998, pp. 4–7.

Whitehouse 2001

David Whitehouse, *Roman Glass in The Corning Museum of Glass*, v. 2, Corning: the museum, 2001.

Whitehouse 2002

D. Whitehouse, "Two Medieval Drinking Glasses with Gilded and Enamelled Ornament," in

G. Kordas, ed., *1st International Conference, Hyalos, Vitrum, Glass: History, Technology and Conservation of Glass and Vitreous Materials in the Hellenic World*, Athens: Glasnet Publications, 2002, pp. 199–203.

Whitehouse 2003

David Whitehouse, *Roman Glass in The Corning Museum of Glass*, v. 3, Corning: the museum, 2003.

Whitehouse 2004

David Whitehouse, "Foreword," in Jutta-Annette Page and others, *Beyond Venice: Glass in Venetian Style, 1500–1750*, Corning: The Corning Museum of Glass, 2004, pp. ii–vi.

Williams 2003

C. K. Williams II, "Frankish Corinth: An Overview," in *Corinth: Results of Excavations Conducted by the American School of Classical Studies at Athens*, v. 20, *Corinth: The Centenary, 1896–1996*, ed. C. K. Williams II and N. Bookidis, Princeton, New Jersey: the school, 2003, pp. 423–434.

Whitehouse 2010

David Whitehouse, *Islamic Glass in The Corning Museum of Glass*, v. 1, Corning: the museum, 2010.

Williams and Zervos 1993

Charles K. Williams and Orestes H. Zervos, "Frankish Corinth: 1992," *Hesperia*, v. 62, no. 1, 1993, pp. 1–52.

Williams and Zervos 1995

Charles K. Williams and Orestes H. Zervos, "Frankish Corinth: 1994," *Hesperia*, v. 64, no. 1, January–March 1995, pp. 1–60.

Zecchin 1987–90

Luigi Zecchin, *Vetro e vetrai di Murano: Studi sulla storia del vetro*, 3 vv., Venice: Arsenale, 1987–1990.

Picture Credits

THE CORNING MUSEUM OF GLASS and the authors thank the following providers for their kind permission to reproduce photographs: Michael Slade and Liam Schaefer at Art Resource, New York City; Paolo Vian at Biblioteca Apostolica Vaticana, Vatican City; Thomas Haggerty and Maria Murguia-Harding at The Bridgeman Art Library International, New York City; Martin Mintz and Auste Mickunaite at The British Library, London; Patrick Andrist at Burgerbibliothek Bern, Bern, Switzerland; Sylvia Hahn at Diözesanmuseum Freising, Freising, Germany; Jacklyn Burns at The J. Paul Getty Museum, Los Angeles; Dedo von Kerssenbrock-Krosigk at Glasmuseum Hentrich, Museum Kunst Palast, Düsseldorf; John-Paul Philippart at Grand Curtius, Glass Department, Liège, Belgium; Ulrike Klotter and Chris Gebel at Landesmuseum Württemberg, Stuttgart; Marion Nickel, Dr. Christian Peitz, and Natascha Vogt at LVR-LandesMuseum Bonn, Bonn; Gérald Machurez at Musée des Beaux-Arts, Chartres; Sandra Schwarz at Museum für Angewandte Kunst Frankfurt, Frankfurt am Main; Joachim Hiltmann and Christine Kitzlinger at Museum für Kunst und Gewerbe Hamburg, Hamburg; Arianne Dannacher at Museum zu Allerheiligen, Schaffhausen, Switzerland; Ingrid Knauf at Museumslandschaft Hessen Kassel, Kassel, Germany; Peter Rohowsky at Picture Desk Inc., New York City; Siv Falk at Statens Historiska Museum, Stockholm; Anna Voellner at Universitätsbibliothek Heidelberg, Heidelberg; and Catherine Draycott at the Wellcome Library, London.

Numbers refer to pages. All photographs are by The Corning Museum of Glass, with the exception of the following:

The Art Archive, photo © Alfredo Dagli Orti: 31, 32, 61 (fig. 24).

The Art Archive, photo © Gianni Dagli Orti: 18, 35, 36 (fig. 5), 37 (fig. 6), 54 (fig. 19), 58, 62.

Erich Lessing/Art Resource, NY: 53.

Image copyright © The Metropolitan Museum of Art/Art Resource, NY: 105, 113, 114, 149, 150, 151, 152.

Réunion des Musées Nationaux/Art Resource, NY, photo © R. J. Ojeda: 34; photo © Hervé Lewandowski: 232.

Scala/Art Resource, NY: 37 (fig. 7), 38, 61 (fig. 23).

© 2010 Biblioteca Apostolica Vaticana: 29.

Bibliothèque Nationale de France: 12.

Alinari/The Bridgeman Art Library: 39.

Giraudon/The Bridgeman Art Library: 44.

National Gallery, London, U.K./The Bridgeman Art Library: 57.

© British Library Board. All Rights Reserved: 15, 17, 24, 43, 54 (fig. 18), 70.

© Copyright The Trustees of The British Museum, London: 41, 49 (fig. 14).

Burgerbibliothek Bern: 60.

Ann Cady: 76, 77.

© Diözesanmuseum Freising, Germany, photo Hermann Reichenwallner: 122, 146, 182.

The J. Paul Getty Museum: 49 (fig. 16).

Glasmuseum Hentrich, Museum Kunst Palast: 140, 179; photo © Saša Fuis, Cologne: 124, 134, 137, 166, 202, 213; photo © Horst Kolberg: 126, 128, 132, 135, 141, 144, 147, 148, 153, 155, 157, 160, 161, 165, 168, 169, 170, 171, 172, 178, 184, 188, 190, 192, 194, 195, 197, 198, 199, 200, 203, 208, 211, 214, 215, 218, 222, 224, 237.

Grand Curtius, Glass Department, photo © Marc Verpoorten: 154.

Fotos: P. Frankenstein, H. Zwietasch, Landesmuseum Württemberg, Stuttgart: 145, 162.

LVR-LandesMuseum Bonn, photo, Hans-Theo Gerhards, LVR-Museumsverbund: 131, 143, 173, 175, 176, 186, 189, 193, 196, 207, 235.

P. Marzari, 88–89.

Musée des Beaux-Arts, Chartres: 230.

Museum für Angewandte Kunst Frankfurt, photo © U. Dettmar: 123, 136, 139, 174.

Museum für Kunst und Gewerbe Hamburg: 183, 206.

Museum zu Allerheiligen, Schaffhausen, photo Müller, Neuhausen am Rheinfall: 129, 130, 187.

Museumslandschaft Hessen Kassel: 47.

Private collection, Germany: 49 (fig. 15).

Mike Schwartz: 74, 78–82.

Statens Historiska Museum, Stockholm, photo © Bengt A. Lundberg: 118.

Universitätsbibliothek Heidelberg: 6, 36 (fig. 4).

Wellcome Library, London: 14.

Index

double *Scheuern. See Doppelscheuern*
Dover, U.K., 107
dragon-stem goblet, 87, 252–253
Dresden, Germany, 233
drinking horn(s), 25, 27, 28, 76
Drudewenshusen, Germany, 64, 67
Düsseldorf, Germany, 19, 124, 134, 137, 140, 160, 167, 179, 202, 213

E

eagle(s), 48, 51, 52
East, Latin, 50, 51
economy, medieval, 10
Edessa, Syria, 11
Edirne, Turkey, 8
Effects of Good Government, 153
Egypt, 11, 21, 46, 50, 55, 63, 66, 84
Eifel region (Germany), 68
Eigelstein, Germany, 163
Emilia-Romagna, Italy, 133
emporium(s), 28, 29, 30
enameling (of glass), 41, 42, 45, 46–48, 53, 69, 73, 83, 84, 85, 153, 154, 226, 231, 233, 234, 243, 245, 254
England, 8, 9, 10, 15, 18, 19, 20, 25, 27, 28, 37, 55, 63, 64, 68, 107, 108, 214; Anglo-Saxon, 16; eastern, 26; southeastern, 27
English Channel, 30
engraving (of glass), 23, 49, 87, 114. *See also* diamond-point engraving
Essex, U.K., 27
Estate Abrau, 149, 150, 151, 152
Eure-et-Loire, France, 231
Europe, 7, 8, 9, 10, 11, 12, 13, 14, 19, 20, 25, 27, 30, 31, 36, 42, 48, 50, 51, 55, 56, 57, 58, 59, 63, 66, 68, 69, 84, 87, 119, 134, 150, 151, 153, 179, 210, 214, 228, 231, 234, 238, 239, 248, 253; central, 33, 37, 42, 45, 50, 51, 52, 66, 127, 211; continental, 9, 111; eastern, 51; northern, 16, 19, 55; northwestern, 68; rural, 10; southern, 8, 53, 124; western, 7, 10, 11, 28, 30, 38, 40, 48, 50, 55, 74, 76, 82, 112, 118, 156
ewer, 37, 244, 248–249, 250–251
expansion of Roman Empire. *See* Roman Empire, expansion of
experimental science. *See* science, experimental
Eyck, Jan van, 57

F

façon de Venise, 45, 248, 253
fairs, 11, 12
Fatimids, 50

Faversham, England, 26, 108
fern-ash glasses, 68
fin molding. *See* insertion molding
finger cup. *See* cup, finger
Fish, Christopher, Collection, 250
fleurs-de-lis, 135, 154
Florence, Italy, 11, 37, 38, 60, 245
forest glass, 20, 33, 42–45, 56, 123, 146, 159, 163, 170, 174, 187, 190, 198, 204; workshop, 43, 71, 159. *See also Waldglas*
France, 8, 11, 15, 19, 20, 27, 37, 55, 56, 59, 64, 68, 104, 110, 111, 112, 123, 135, 141, 143, 231, 254; eastern, 45, 142; northeastern, 26, 27, 36, 140; northern, 12, 20, 25, 27, 28, 104, 105, 107, 115, 147, 148, 156, 159; north-western, 9, 147; southern, 134; southwestern, 56
Franconia, Germany, 41
Frankfurt am Main, Germany, 42, 123, 136, 139, 174
Franks, 8
Frederick II (emperor), 51
free blowing, 37, 71
Freiburg, Germany, 134
Freising, Germany, 122, 146, 182
Fulda, Germany, 63
funnel beaker. *See* beaker(s), funnel
furnace(s), 15, 20, 21, 31, 45, 63, 66, 68, 69, 73, 75, 77, 78, 80; tank, 21
fusing (of glass), 22, 71, 96, 250
Fustāt (Old Cairo), Egypt, 50, 66

G

Gasparetto, Astone, 40
Gaul, 8
Gemäldegalerie. *See* Staatliche Museen zu Berlin
Genoa, Italy, 11, 17
Geoffrey (abbot), 56
Germanic peoples, 8
Germany, 10, 20, 25, 27, 28, 29, 31, 33, 36, 40, 42, 44, 45, 46, 49, 50, 55, 56, 59, 63, 64, 66, 67, 68, 82, 85, 104, 107, 110, 111, 112, 113, 114, 122, 123, 126, 127, 128, 129, 130, 131, 132, 134, 135, 136, 137, 138, 139, 140, 141, 142, 143, 144, 145, 146, 147, 149, 150, 151, 153, 155, 156, 159, 160, 163, 164, 167, 169, 170, 171, 173, 174, 175, 176, 177, 178, 179, 180, 181, 182, 183, 184, 185, 186, 187, 188, 189, 190, 191, 192, 193, 194, 195, 196, 197, 198, 199, 200, 201, 202, 203, 204, 205, 206, 207, 208, 209, 210, 211, 212, 213, 214, 215, 216, 219, 220, 223, 225, 228, 233, 237, 243; northern, 42, 55, 142; northwestern, 9, 29; southern, 33, 113, 122, 125, 141, 142, 144, 186, 193; southwestern, 176, 204; western, 147
Getty, J. Paul, Museum (Los Angeles), 49, 100
Ghent, Belgium, 44

International Association for the History of Glass, 19
Iran, 8, 50, 55, 110, 233; northeastern, 124
Iraq, 8
Islam, 8
Islamic: gilded and enameled glass, 42, 46–48, 231, 233; workshop(s), 73, 82; world, 20, 45, 46, 50, 53, 55, 58, 59, 214, 228, 234, 238, 239
Israel, 21, 64, 99
Israel Antiquities Authority, 99
Israel Museum (Jerusalem), 99
Italy, 7, 8, 9, 10, 19, 28, 30, 37, 38, 40, 42, 46, 50, 58, 60, 63, 64, 68, 85, 87, 93, 119, 122, 123, 125, 126, 127, 135, 141, 153, 154, 179, 226, 234, 236; central, 33, 34, 48, 53, 59, 61, 152, 233; northern, 61, 84, 125, 133, 144, 234; southern, 30, 50, 51, 59

J

Jáchymov, Bohemia, 197
jacks, 73, 74, 78, 79, 80, 82, 83
Jacques de Vitry (bishop), 50, 51
James (saint), 56
Jantzen Collection, 137
jars, 28
Jerome (saint), 172
Jerusalem, Israel, 11, 53, 99
Jesus Christ. *See* Christ
Joachimsthal. *See* Jáchymov
John (saint), 13
John I Tzimisces (emperor), 50
John the Baptist, 38
Journal of Glass Studies, 19
jug(s), 69, 245
Justus of Ghent, 44
Jutes, 8

K

Kassel, Germany, 47, 82
Kempston beakers. *See* beaker(s), Kempston
Kendenich, Germany, 173
Kent, England, 26, 108; kings of, 108
Kerch, Ukraine, 99
Keulenglas(äser). *See* beaker(s), club-shaped
kick(s), 28, 34, 37, 44, 73–76, 80, 122
King's Field, 108
Kirby, F. M., Foundation, 247
Kloster zu Allerheiligen (Schaffhausen), 130
Knaresborough, U.K. Castle, 53
knotsbeker. *See* beaker(s), club-shaped
Kosovo, 141
Kouchakji Collection, 100

Krautstrunk(ünke), 44, 146, 183, 184, 185, 186, 187, 188, 189, 190, 191, 192, 193
Krefeld, Germany, 126, 128, 132, 135, 141, 144, 147, 148, 153, 155, 156, 160, 164, 169, 170, 171, 172, 178, 184, 188, 190, 192, 194, 195, 197, 198, 199, 200, 203, 208, 211, 214, 215, 219, 223, 225, 237
Krefeld-Gellep, Germany, 27
Krueger, Ingeborg, 42, 68
Kuttrolf(e), 45, 211, 212, 213

L

La Plaine, France, 12
La Seube, France, 134
Lagoon, Venetian, 84, 141
Lamm, Carl Johan, 42, 47, 48
lamp(s), 19, 23, 28, 30, 47, 52, 53–55, 56, 84, 214; hanging, 23, 47, 53, 55, 95; mosque, 47, 48, 53
land tenure, 10
Landesmuseum Württemberg (Stuttgart), 42, 136, 145, 163
Lanna Collection, 145, 183
Last Supper, 33, 133
Last Supper, 34, 216
Latin East. *See* East, Latin
Laudengrund, Germany. glasshouse, 67
lead glass, 68–69
legends/literature, glass in, 7, 13–16
Lek (river), 30
Lendit Fair, 12
lenses, 13, 57, 60–61
Leo II (pope), 236
Leo III (pope), 9
Leo IV (pope), 55
Leo X (pope), 245
Leutkirch, Germany, 186
Levant, 11, 42, 51, 63, 99; raw glass exported from, 21, 51, 52
"Liber ad honorem Augusti," 55, 60
lid, 224–225
Lieberstein, von, family, 41
Liège, Belgium, 104, 171
"lily pad" decoration, 201
"linen smoother(s)," 68, 119
lion(s), 48, 50, 51, 52, 228; masks, 247
lions' heads, 85
literature, glass in. *See* legends/literature, glass in
Lochnerin, Katerina, 85, 243
Lombards, 8, 9
London, England, 56; U.K., 13, 14, 15, 17, 41, 43, 49, 54, 57, 71, 99, 108, 138, 231
Lorenzetti, Ambrogio, 153

pope, Medici, 245
Populonia bottle, 92–93
Portner family, 41
potash glasses, 51
Pozzuoli, Italy, 93
Prague: Bohemia, 214; Czech Republic, 155
Provence, France, 61
Provins, France, 12
prunted beaker. *See* beaker(s), decorated with prunts
prunts, 36, 44, 69, 72, 124, 125, 126, 127, 128, 129, 130,
    131, 132, 146, 149, 150, 152, 155, 171, 178, 182, 184, 186,
    187, 191, 195, 198, 204, 206, 219, 247; claw, 72
Purgatorio (Dante), 15
Puteoli, Italy, 23

Q

Qur'an, 13

R

Rademacher, Franz, 19, 105, 202, 204
Rainham, U.K., 27
Raqqa, Syria, 48
Ratzeburg, Germany, 139
Ravenna, Italy, 133
reading glasses. *See* spectacles
receiver (distilling apparatus), 59, 237, 238, 239
Regensburg, Germany, 140
Reichenbach, Germany, 176
relics, 10, 18, 51, 55, 56, 173, 185, 234; cult of, 56
reliquary(ies), 10, 16, 20, 28, 52, 55–56, 114, 236
Renaissance, 7, 8, 9, 20, 83, 84–87, 241–255
Restormel Castle, U.K., 42
reticello: canes, 29, 30; trails, 29
Revelation, Book of, 13, 14
Rheinisches Landesmuseum Bonn. *See* LVR-
    Landesmuseum Bonn
Rhine (river), 11, 30, 69
Rhineland, 25, 27, 104; middle, 147
Rijksmuseum (Amsterdam), 194
Ring(el)becher. *See* beaker(s), ring
rock crystal, 50, 52, 55, 83, 85, 197
Roger of Helmarshausen, 31
Roman Catholic Church, 154, 234
Roman Empire, 7, 16, 21; eastern, 8; expansion of, 7;
    fall of, 7; western, 8
Roman glass/glassmaking, 23, 30, 63, 64, 73; late, 20
Roman period/world, 19, 21, 23, 45, 63, 71, 85, 211;
    late, 21, 55, 56, 115, 160
Rome: ancient, 7, 8, 10, 20, 21, 22, 23, 71, 91–101, 214;
    Italy, 97, 154, 236

Romulus Augustulus (emperor), 8
rooster, 110
rosolio, 58
Rottenburg, Germany, 176, 185
Rotterdam, the Netherlands, 19, 160
Rouen, France, 15, 19, 147
roulette, 72, 167
roundel(s), 22, 46, 226
Royal Ontario Museum (Toronto), 20
Rüsselbecher. *See* beaker(s), claw
Russia, 149, 150, 151, 152
Russian Imperial Apanages, 149, 150, 151, 152

S

Sabellico, Marcantonio, 244
sacred spaces, vessels used in, 20, 33, 52–56
Sady, Czech Republic. Staré Město, 64, 67
Saint Bavo's Cathedral (Ghent), 44
Saint Mark, Basilica of (Venice), 90
Saint Martin, church of (Leutkirch), 186
Saint Nicolas d'Oignies, monastery of (Namur), 50
Saint-Denis, France, 12, 56
Saint-Genest (Nevers), 56
saints, 10, 55, 56, 185
Saladin, 11
Salerno, Italy, 59
Salerno Medical School. *See* Schola Medica
    Salernitana
salicornia, 69
San Gimignano, Italy. Cathedral of, 39
San Giorgio in Velabro, Church of (Rome), 236
San Nicolò, convent of (Treviso), 61
San Vincenzo al Volturno, Italy, 30; Benedictine
    monastery of, 28, 30
Sandro di Popozo, 60
Sangiorgi Collection, 96
Santa Croce (Florence), 37
Santa Margherita, Church of (Orvieto), 233
Santa Maria Novella (Florence), 38
Santiago de Compostela, Spain, 56
Saranda Kolones (castle near Paphos), 46
Sasanians, 8
Satan, 85, 243
Saxons, 8, 16
Scandinavia, 9, 19, 20, 25, 28, 29, 30, 42, 119
Schaffhausen, Switzerland, 129, 130, 140, 187
Scheuer(n), 45, 73, 142, 144, 145, 197, 198, 199, 215, 216,
    222–223; stoneware, 198
Schiffton, H., Collection, 201
Schmidt, Robert, 42
Schnütgen Collection, 183